THE WESLEYAN THEOLOGY SERIES

I0202086

Jesus Christ

T.A.
Noble

f·

THE FOUNDRY
PUBLISHING·

The Foundry Publishing®
PO Box 419527
Kansas City, MO 64141
thefoundrypublishing.com

ISBN: 978-0-8341-4313-5

Printed in the
United States of America

Cover design: Arthur Cherry
Interior design: Sharon Page

Library of Congress Cataloging-in-Publication Data
A complete catalog record for this book is available from the Library of Congress.

10 9 8 7 6 5 4 3 2 1

Contents

Prefatory Note

The Wesleyan Theology Series would not be complete without a book on Jesus Christ, the centre of our faith. To supply this, the publisher has requested that I produce a précis or summary of Parts 1 and 2 of *The Grace of Our Lord Jesus Christ*, which is the first volume of *Christian Theology*, published in 2022. This book therefore includes some passages taken word for word from that volume along with other passages written to summarize other material. *Christian Theology* is written mainly for students completing a master's degree although intended to be readable for the interested Christian public. This shorter summary may be useful for those who need a simpler introduction or who cannot devote time to the longer volume. Any reader who needs fuller references than are given here will find them in the longer volume.

—T.A. Noble
Nazarene Theological College
Manchester
February 2024

Introduction:
The 'Who?' Question

Asking questions is the key to understanding. Small children will ask 'Why?' questions all day long! But that is how they learn.

What are the important questions for us as Christians? Like children in our Father's house, we want answers. We want to know and understand. So it is good for us to have lots of questions.

- How can we know God?
- How can we be saved?
- How do we get to heaven?
- Who will be saved?
- Has God predetermined who will be saved?
- Why did God permit evil?
- What is God's plan for the end times?
- What is baptism for?
- How does God guide us?

We could go on and on! But it is good to have such questions. They show that we are intellectually alive and thinking. It is when we are puzzled by something that we are ready to learn and grow in understanding.

Jesus knew that. That is why he puzzled the disciples and the crowds again and again. He didn't explain things in a boring, matter-of-fact way. He teased and provoked people with his parables. He made them think! Perhaps the key to his teaching method is the question he asked Simon Peter: 'What do you think, Simon?' (Matt. 17:25).

It can be helpful to see that there are different kinds of questions. Further, the way we think is shaped by the kinds of questions we typically ask. Long ago, Aristotle suggested that there are basically four kinds of questions: Why? How? What? Whence? Perhaps we may see these as representing different ways of thinking.

Why?

We can think of 'Why?' as the philosophical or intellectual question. It is the question we ask when we are looking for explanations. These explanations can then be formed into elaborate theories and metaphysical systems. This kind of question became characteristic of the culture of ancient Greece, and it has been said that all Western philosophy has been only a footnote on the philosophical thinking of Plato and Aristotle! Other ancient cultures such as those in India and China also wrestled with philosophical questions.

The typical 'Why?' question for Christians is, 'Why did God permit evil and suffering?' We can think of it as the question Jesus asked on the cross: 'My God, my God, why have you forsaken me?' (Matt. 27:46, NIV). Theodicy, questioning why there is evil in God's good creation, is therefore a necessary part of Philosophical Theology. The philosophical mindset is a valuable way of thinking.

But Christian Theology as a whole cannot take the 'Why?' question as its starting point and dominating question. If it does, the Church is reduced to an educational institution, a branch of the academy; sermons are turned into lectures, and church meetings into seminars. We become philosophers rather than theologians, our thinking devoted to our own theories and explanations rather than seeking to be obedient to the Word of God. Philosophy is a good servant for the Christian theologian, but a bad master. Rather, we need to recognize that all 'Why?' questions emerge from an already existing framework of assumptions, whereas repentance at its deepest level is precisely the questioning of our own questions.

There is therefore a deeper kind of question that we need to ask.

How?

We can think of 'How?' as the technological question. This is typical of those who think of themselves as practical people and may even despise intellectual questions or debate! This kind of question was typical of the ancient Romans, the great pragmatists whose feats of engineering and military organization made them masters of the Mediterranean world. Today such technological thinking is dominant in our culture, particularly in the Western world.

'How?' questions, like 'Why?' questions, are good questions to ask in Christian Theology. How shall we evangelize? How shall we organize the Church and make it grow? How shall we preach and pray and worship the Lord? These are important questions of Practical Theology.

But Christian Theology as a whole cannot start from or be centred on such questions, necessary though they are. The temptations here are subtle. But if the pragmatic mindset dominates, the Church becomes merely an efficient business, evangelism degenerates into a spiritual sales drive, and we can even depersonalize those we seek to win for the sake of growth. The 'How?' questions are legitimate and vital and necessary, but they must not be the be-all and end-all of our thinking.

When this kind of thinking dominates in the realm of Christian doctrine, it can produce a kind of depersonalizing technology of salvation. It may not be coincidence that it was a Roman who asked the question, 'What must I do to be saved?' (Acts 16:30). And even where we recognize that we can do nothing but believe in Christ, we can still try to produce a technological explanation, a 'theory' of 'how' the Atonement works.

Once again, there is a deeper question we need to ask.

Who?

Aristotle's other two questions were 'What?' and 'Whence?' These may be seen as the scientific questions: What is this thing? Where does it come from? What is it made of? Of course, science must not be confused with technology. We are not thinking of applied science here, but of pure science. Pure scientific research will no doubt have practical consequences, but that is not its goal. Its goal is to understand some reality for its own sake and to respect its own integrity.

When the reality we seek to know is personal, then the 'What?' and 'Whence?' questions become 'Who?' And in the Humanities and the human sciences it is vital to understand that the 'Who?' question implies respect and indeed reverence. True knowledge of our friends is not in order to answer metaphysical questions about them, and certainly not to make use of them for our pragmatic ends. We come to *know* them (and this is fully *cognitive*) as we interact in the story or drama of our lives.

So in Christian Theology, the primary question is the 'Who?' question. This is not merely a modern question. This is the great question of the Bible. It is Moses' question at the burning bush: 'What is your name?' or, in other words, 'Who are you?' (see Exod. 3:13). It is the great question of the Psalms in the worship of the temple: 'Who is the King of glory?' (Ps. 24:8, 10). It is the key question Jesus asked the disciples: 'Who do you say that I am?' (Mark 8:29). And it is the key question Paul asked at his conversion: 'Who are you, Lord?' (Acts 9:5).

Being 'saved' is not merely a technological process—following instructions on the packet, a psychological happening, a commercial transaction, or inducing a certain kind of spiritual crisis. It is not merely adopting certain beliefs. True conversion is coming *to know a Person* and entering into a relationship with *him*.

When the Church is centred on the 'Who?' question, then it is not reduced to an educational institution or a business venture or commercial sales drive, but it is centred on worship. 'Why?' questions and 'How?' questions have their important place, but at the centre of our life as a community we seek to understand more profoundly 'Who' God is. Our life is centred on our 'gathering' as the 'assembly' of God to hear his Word in faith and to respond in confession and in prayer and worship. Then indeed the Church is the Church.

Dietrich Bonhoeffer insisted in his lectures on Christology, the doctrine of Christ, that the 'Who?' question was the key question.[1] And to explore ever more deeply the question, 'Who is God?' we must ask, 'Who are you, Lord?'

The Point of Access

It is not enough to know doctrines or theories. It is not enough to know practices and follow them. What is at the heart of the faith is *to know God*. This is not just sub-personal knowledge *about* God. This is Person-to-person knowledge *of* God.

This Person-to-person knowledge comes personally, but not individualistically. It comes through the community of the Church. It comes through God's self-revelation through the prophets and apostles in inspired Holy Scripture. The apostolic Gospel embodied in the New Testament gives us the definitive interpretation of the prophetic word in the Old Testament. The preaching of the Word in the Church is therefore central.

But to know God it is not enough to be present when the Church gathers, and it is not even enough to know the Bible by heart. Bible and Church are essential. But God's self-revelation is centred in the Person of his beloved Son, the Word made flesh. We 'come to the Father thro' Jesus, the Son.'[2]

Paul puts this so helpfully when he writes that 'through him we both [Jews and gentiles] have access in one Spirit to the Father' (Eph. 2:18). If we want to know God, Christ is the point of access. By the Spirit we come to God in and through him. That is why Christology, the doctrine of Christ, is so vital.

In this book, therefore, we are addressing the question, 'Who is Jesus?'

The Plan

For the last several centuries, scholars have been trying to answer that key question by employing the technique of History—the so-called historical-critical method. Christians cannot object to that since we believe that Jesus is fully hu-

---

1. Dietrich Bonhoeffer, *Christology* (London: Collins, 1966), 30ff.

2. Fanny J. Crosby, 'To God Be the Glory', in *Sing to the Lord* (Kansas City: Lillenas, 1993), no. 36.

man. The critical methods of historical study can therefore say something about him. In a 'Prelude', therefore, comprising the first two chapters, we shall recount this attempt to understand Jesus via this method.

But when we come to the evidence for his resurrection, we have to face the question whether this whole method can bring us to know this Person. The evidence points to his rising from the dead, but if that is true, then the so-called historical-critical method cannot take us any further. We are challenged to put our faith in this risen Lord and to listen to the witnesses he appointed. We have come to the threshold of faith and commitment. The enigma of the resurrection of Jesus forces us to decide either to be believers or sceptics. We are challenged to fall at his feet with Thomas and confess, 'My Lord and my God!' (John 20:28).

In Part I, therefore, comprising Chapters 3 to 6, we shall consider the answer that Christians give out of their faith in the risen Lord. We can no longer pretend to be 'neutral', but pass to that true objectivity only possible for those who recognize the Truth. We move on from this historical 'Prelude' to consider the Church's doctrine that arose from divine revelation. No longer will we operate as historians who see with natural human insight and wisdom ('the eye of the flesh'), but now with new insight given by the Spirit, exploring our faith in Jesus as Lord.

In Chapter 3, entitled 'Jesus Revealed in the Gospel', we shall explore the apostolic proclamation. We find this embedded in the New Testament, which grew out of it. As we shall see, the Gospel is a short narrative composed of two episodes: Christ died for our sins, and Christ rose from the dead. This one-in-two story of the Gospel of crucifixion and resurrection may be seen to be at the root of all the New Testament books and is the clue to their interpretation. The full humanity of our Lord is seen in his life of service and, most profoundly, in his suffering and death on the cross. His full deity is revealed in his resurrection. But, given that this man was God all along, then it is necessary to speak of Incarnation. It is God who has taken our flesh to share in our suffering and so to raise us up with him from death and destruction. We must therefore visualize a full parabolic movement of descent from eternity to death and ascension from death to eternity.

In Chapter 4, we shall examine the defence of this Gospel by the early bishops and teachers of the Church, particularly the great Irenaeus, bishop of Lyons. These Church 'Fathers' (as they are known) encountered those who distorted the truth by *denying* the full deity or the full humanity of Christ. And to distort the Gospel is to deny Christ and to deny our salvation. This is not just a cosy abstract debate but a matter of life and death.

In Chapter 5, we shall examine the great defence of the faith of the Church by the 'Later Fathers' as it was under threat from those who *compromised* the full deity of Christ or his full humanity. We shall see how the Church formulated the great Nicene Creed and the Symbol of Chalcedon to safeguard the truth of the New Testament Gospel. In Chapter 6, we shall turn to the debates during and following the Evangelical Reformation and the doctrine of the leaders in the later Evangelical awakening, particularly the Wesleys.

Part II will consider the doctrine of Christ as we face the challenges of the later modern era. Chapter 7 will look at the attempt of the 'Liberal' tradition to meet modern challenges. Chapter 8 will consider four leading figures who rejected these attempts and who tried to re-express the doctrine in the modern context. Chapter 9 will examine questions arising as we try to wrestle today with the full deity and the full humanity of our Lord, looking at contemporary attempts to 'contextualize' the doctrine. Chapter 10 will conclude by trying to see how these two, deity and humanity, are one in the Person of our Lord Jesus Christ. As a divine 'Person', constituted by his relations with the Father in the Spirit, he draws us into relationship with him in the Spirit by which we become truly 'personal'. We are called to relate to him personally in faith as the one unique Person, truly God, truly human, but one Lord Jesus Christ.

The 'Historical' Jesus

ONE

The Historical Approach to Jesus

For the last three centuries, scholars have been trying to understand who Jesus is through historical research. That seems reasonable! Here is a man who lived twenty centuries ago; how else would we understand who he was and what he did?

As Christians, we cannot object to this. After all, Christians believe that Jesus was a man, truly a human being who lived at a certain time in a certain place. We may believe more than that about him, but we certainly believe that! So we cannot object to using historical research.

But this is where we have to be careful. We need to note carefully that the so-called historical-critical method with its techniques of historical research arose itself in a certain cultural and historical context—the European 'Enlightenment'. We cannot assume that it is a completely objective tool. Postmodernity questions that 'modern' assumption. Rather, we have to understand the context in which the modern discipline of History arose—the Enlightenment and the rise of Deism. In a few pages we can summarize that context with a quick tour. We shall come to the search for the 'historical' Jesus shortly, but first, in a couple of pages we must sketch the philosophical assumptions behind it.

The Enlightenment

The word 'modern' was coined in the sixteenth century to refer to the era beginning in the fifteenth-century Renaissance when European artists and thinkers believed themselves to be witnessing the 'rebirth' of the ancient classical civilization of Greece and Rome. This led to the birth of what we now call 'Modern Science' in the work of Francis Bacon (1561–1626) and of 'Modern Philosophy' in the work of the French philosopher René Descartes (1596–1650).

Descartes proposed the 'method of doubt', doubting everything he could in order to discover what was certain knowledge. He came to the conclusion that the only thing he could not doubt was that, even if he was deceived about everything, he had to exist in order to be deceived. This was his famous *cogito ergo sum*, 'I think, therefore I am.' From this supposedly secure basis (himself!), he thought he could *deduce* the existence of God and therefore be certain that there was a real world around him. He thought that this brought the absolute certainty he craved, and a school of philosophy arose from this, known as *rationalism*. In fact, however, Descartes' version of the 'ontological argument' for the existence of God, that the *concept* of God *required* that he exist, just as the concept of a triangle required that its angles add up to 180 degrees, remains controversial.

In Britain, a different school of thought developed. It also looked for certainty and began with the subjective thinking of the individual, but it proposed that all knowledge came to the individual's mind from the five senses. Genuine knowledge arose not by *deductive logic* but by *inductive logic*. If I observe that A always follows B (as far as I can observe it), then it probably always will. This did not provide absolute certainty, but a level of knowledge 'beyond all reasonable doubt'. John Locke (1632–1704) and Sir Isaac Newton (1642–1727) were the two major thinkers in the development of what became known as *empiricism*, and it was closely linked to the rise of modern science.

Deism

What concerns us about these developments was the way in which they led to the rise of Deism. Deism did not appear to be a new religion, but simply a more rational way of talking about God. It was assumed that all monotheistic religions were talking about the same God. Now the Newtonian cosmology, which had captured the imagination of the whole culture, was pointing toward a rational God who had created the universe as a great machine rather like the recently perfected mechanism of the clock. God was therefore the first cause or designer of the universe. Blaise Pascal (1623-62), the French philosopher and mathematician, clearly saw a vitally important difference when he contrasted 'the God of Abraham, Isaac, and Jacob' with 'the god of the philosophers'. But it was the latter that now dominated European thought. Those parts of Christian belief that were based not on 'Reason' or 'Natural Theology' but on biblical revelation were marginalized or completely dismissed.

It is important to realize that this was the cultural context in which historical investigation into the life of Jesus began. In Germany, Christian Wolff (1679–1754) was a disciple of the rationalism that began with Descartes and was continued by the German philosopher Gottfried Leibniz (1646–1716). And it was Leibniz's philosophy that strongly influenced H.S. Reimarus (1694–1768), who initiated the first attempt to subject the figure of Jesus to historical inquiry.

Reimarus was a schoolteacher and a strong advocate of 'natural' religion. 'Reason' leads us to believe in an eternal creator and the immortality of the human soul, but the mysteries and miracles of revealed, biblical religion could be dismissed. The Bible is full of irrational and incredible stories; the Old Testament knows nothing of the immortality of the soul and is ethically barbaric, while the writers of the New Testament had perpetrated a fraud. He speculated that Jesus was a Jewish revolutionary who failed and was crucified, but his disciples made up the story of his resurrection for their own ends. Reimarus was not a historian. He examined no sources, nor did he use the historical-critical method. He simply rejected much of the Bible because of his Deism. He kept his views secret, but after his death, his writings were published by the deist G.E. Lessing (1729-81).

Lessing inherited the Platonist divorce between the world of eternal truths and the world of accidental events. He claimed therefore that there was an 'ugly ditch' between the 'eternal truths of reason' and the 'accidental truths of history'. It was absurd to think that Eternal Truth could become incarnate in the lower realm of history. History could not be the way to truth, and Jesus of Nazareth was a Jewish revolutionary or, at best, a teacher of Ethics.

The Enlightenment Stumbles

But the high Enlightenment had the seeds of its own destruction germinating within it. The razor-sharp mind of the Edinburgh philosopher David Hume (1711-76) questioned the historicity of the biblical miracles, since we could only accept as true and factual those events that were in 'analogy' with our own uniform experience. With no experience of miracles, we had to assume that the 'laws of nature' were never violated. But significantly, Hume also questioned the foundations of Deism by undermining the arguments for the existence of God. He also cast doubt on the notion of causality, which was a necessary assumption of the empirical scientific method, and also on the idea of the soul or self. The methodology of doubt was leading to the abyss of scepticism. Hume was opposed by Thomas Reid (1710-96), a minister of the Church of Scotland and a professor first at Aberdeen and then at Glasgow University. He was an exponent of 'Scottish Common Sense Realism', recently defended by Alvin Plantinga and Nicholas Wolterstorff.[1]

On the continent, however, Immanuel Kant (1724–1804) was more influential. Kant was a deist who defended the Enlightenment. Reason, not tradition, was to determine what we could accept as true. But David Hume awakened him from what he regarded as his 'dogmatic slumber' as a deist holding to pure rationalism. He accepted the empiricist view that all our knowledge came through the senses, but he combined that with a doctrine more akin to rationalism, that the human mind organized what it received from raw sense perception with some innate 'categories' of thought. These included space, time, and causality. This meant however that we only know things as they appear to us (the *phenomena*) and never as they really are in themselves (the *noumena*). The 'thing in itself' (*das Ding an sich*) is inaccessible and unknowable. This meant that space and time

1. See Alvin Plantinga and Nicholas Wolterstorff, eds., *Faith and Rationality: Reason and Belief in God* (Notre Dame, IN: University of Notre Dame Press, 1983).

and causation were not objective characteristics of the universe, but merely categories of the human mind. It also meant that the deist arguments for the existence of God as the First Cause (the cosmological argument) and as the Designer (the teleological argument) both failed. God could not be known, since he was not among the *phenomena* that we encountered in the world, but among the *noumena*.

But although Deism appeared to be fatally wounded, Kant enabled it to survive by arguing that one had to postulate the existence of God to explain the objectivity of the moral law. And in the English-speaking world, William Paley (1743–1805) helped Deism to survive by popularizing the 'argument from design' (or 'teleological argument') that just as a watch required a designer, so, too, did the universe and all the complex mechanisms within it.

This very quick review of the eighteenth-century Enlightenment and Deism has now given us the background to the emergence of the discipline of History. But we must note that its 'historical-critical method' was closely tied to a philosophical system of beliefs and assumptions known as 'Historicism'.

The Romantic Movement

Around the turn of the nineteenth century a reaction to the abstract thinking of the Enlightenment took place. It usually goes by the name of the Romantic Movement. In some ways it continued the rationalist and empiricist thinking of the Enlightenment, but in other ways it was a reaction. You could say that it was a kind of 'postmodernism', at once both a continuation of and a reaction against Enlightenment 'modernism'. It burst on the scene during the Revolutionary and Napoleonic Wars with the poetry of Goethe and Wordsworth, the music of Beethoven and Schubert, and the historical novels of Scott. Emotion superseded 'Reason', and love of the romantic past superseded love of the abstract and universal.

The reaction can be seen in the thinking of Kant's colleague Johann Georg Hamann (1730-88), who belonged to the Pietist tradition. In contrast to the use of French as the language of diplomacy and culture, Hamann championed the despised German language and the ancient folk tales, poetry, and songs of Germany. He championed local and national identity over against the French language and claims to universal abstract truth. Gottfried von Herder (1744–1803) took this further. He published the first exposition of what may be called 'Historicist' thought in *Yet Another Philosophy of History* (1774). The universal abstract values of the Enlightenment were rejected in favour of the view that all values were local and historical and therefore multiple. There were no universal abstract norms by which to measure 'progress'. With such a reaction against metaphysics, the discipline or science of History became the primary intellectual endeavour.

Historicism and Schleiermacher

Wilhelm von Humboldt (1767–1835) developed Historicist thinking further. The focus of his thought was the individual person or state that developed according to its own dynamic. Behind the chaos of history was the providential hand of God, but the way to understand the world was not through abstract schemes of universal truth but to focus on the individual person, the individual state, the individual event. One had to seek understanding by an intuitive insight that came through the study of evidence, sources, and original documents. This close study of documents became the basis for the new method of Historiography. Von Humboldt's thinking was also to lead to the development of the new science of interpretation or 'Hermeneutics'.

Historicism was a component in the thinking of Samuel Taylor Coleridge (1772–1834) and Friedrich Schleiermacher (1768–1834), the two religious thinkers most closely associated with Romanticism. For Coleridge, 'Reason' included not only logic and speculative thought but also imagination. Logical argument cannot bring us to God (as Kant had said), but 'Reason' must be expanded to include 'practical reason', which involves our will and conscience and moral being. True rationality included engaging 'nature' with our powers of fancy and imagination and seeing 'nature' in an organic and 'spiritual' light rather than merely as a mechanism. Only when there is this subjective commitment to the truth can objective truth 'find' me.

Schleiermacher accepted that Kant had closed the door not only to rationalist proofs of God's existence but to any attempt by the human mind to reach the sphere of the *noumenal*. He therefore drew on his Pietist upbringing to base his Theology not on biblical or historical revelation, nor on argument or historical evidence, but on 'piety' or 'religion'. For German Pietism (as later for Methodism and Evangelicalism), true piety was that conscious awareness, that feeling of the blessing and presence of God, which came as a result of the preaching of the Gospel of 'Christ crucified'. The Gospel was thus the basis of their theology. Schleiermacher turned this on its head. Not the New Testament Gospel but the piety of religious feeling was the basis of his Theology.

'Religion' and 'the Absolute'

'Religion' was not a matter of response to the proclamation of the cross, nor of proofs and evidence as Deism thought, but was *God-consciousness*. That was a feeling or awareness or consciousness (*Gefühl*) of the Infinite in the finite and the Eternal in the temporal. This preceded all conscious discursive thought and was present in all human beings. Theology therefore made no claim to be the 'science' of God, who was inaccessible in the *noumenal* realm, but was the study of the *phenomena* of human religion or piety. Christianity was one historical form 'religion' took, and in Schleiermacher's view, the most advanced. Christians drew their God-consciousness from the supreme and perfect God-consciousness of Jesus. This was mediated to them through the fellowship of the Church, which he founded. For this reason, Schleiermacher loved to preach from the Gospel of John where he thought he could find evidence of Jesus' own perfect God-consciousness. That was what was of prime interest about Jesus of Nazareth—his own religious consciousness, his own sense of absolute dependence upon God and the effect that had on his followers. This concern to know about Jesus' own 'God-consciousness' was the original motive for what later became called the 'quest' for the 'historical' Jesus.

G.W.F. Hegel (1770–1831), Schleiermacher's fellow professor at the newly founded University of Berlin, was his great rival. Hegel had a different response to Kant. He proposed that we begin with the bold supposition that Ultimate Objective Reality is to be identified with 'Mind'. In other words, God is the Ultimate Subject, or to put that another way, 'The Absolute' is *Geist* (translated as either 'Spirit' or 'Mind'). With this daring speculative move, Hegel revived the apparently fatally wounded tradition of metaphysics by devising the greatest metaphysical system perhaps since Plato. But whereas for Plato's 'Idealism' (as it is known), the Absolute is conceived as static, the eternal upper realm of the Forms, for the new Idealism of Hegel it was dynamic. The Absolute is continually *moving* into the world, realizing itself through world history. This was the true meaning of the picture language of the Christian faith. But this implied that time and history had to be included *within* our doctrine of God in what has since been classified as a kind of 'panentheism'. This, according to Hegel, was the philosophical concept behind the Christian picture language. Everything (*pan*) is within (*en*) God. This could be called a kind of metaphysical Historicism, but its relevance for us is the influence Hegel had upon the scholar who launched what has become known as the 'First Quest' for the Historical Jesus.

The First Quest

David Friedrich Strauss (1808-74) was a student at the University of Berlin influenced by Hegel and also by Historicism. Those two influences came together in his book *Das Leben Jesu* (*The Life of Jesus*), a highly significant and controversial turning point. As a historical study of Jesus, it employed the Historiography of Humboldt, sifting the evidence. But whereas Newton had allowed that God could intervene in the world, the assumption now (inherited from the Deism influenced by Hume) was that God could not or did not intervene. The universe was seen as a closed system of cause and effect, and the idea that God could intervene was regarded as a primitive superstition contrary to 'science'. But far from being implied by objective 'science', it was rather a deist assumption built into the historical-critical method.

Strauss applied this rigorously to the four Gospels. He rejected not only the miracle stories but also what he saw as 'contradictory' accounts and was left with a fairly minimal history: that Jesus was baptized by John, that he had a band of disciples, and that he believed that he was the Messiah. Under the influence of the prophecy of the suffering Servant in Isaiah, he had believed that he would be killed but would return as the exalted Son of Man. But the birth narratives, the transfiguration, the triumphal entry into Jerusalem, and all the miracle stories were fictional. Most significantly, that meant that the resurrection had not happened and that Jesus was misled by the superstitious views of his time.

Strauss, however, had a more positive view of the 'fictions' in the Gospels than Reimarus. They were not deliberate deceit by the disciples. Rather, he saw them as 'myths' that were simply ways in which people in ancient culture expressed their ideas, since they were incapable of distinguishing those from 'history' (what really happened). Strauss recognized that his historical scepticism would be devastating for Christian believers. But he thought that belief in God could be re-expressed in terms provided by Hegel. The Person of Christ was no longer central. He was not literally the 'God-man'. But he held a unique place because he was the illustration (*Vorstellung*) of the philosophical concept (*Begriff*) that divinity and humanity were one. The human race as a whole was the incarnation of deity. *Der Geist*, the great Mind or Spirit, the Absolute, was realizing itself through the human race in the whole of world history. Although Strauss's career was ruined by the controversy he ignited, his teacher F.C. Baur developed a school of thought at the University of Tübingen. They quietly pursued historical-critical research, comparing the Gospel of John with the Synoptics, for example, and concluding that it was not historically reliable.

Opposition to the 'Quest'

After Strauss, numerous attempts were made to write biographies of Jesus. We may note as an example the very popular and highly romanticized (but also anti-Semitic) life story written by Ernest Renan, *Vie de Jésus*, published in 1863. More a novel than a biography, it portrayed Jesus preaching 'a sweet theology of love'. Like many of the others, it was historically worthless. Significant historical work was done, however, by Johannes Weiss, who drew attention to the importance of Jesus' eschatology, his preaching of the end times. Jesus was not some kind of social reformer or teacher of ethics (as his father-in-law, the theologian Albrecht Ritschl, tended to portray him), but a strange Jewish prophet declaring the imminent end of the world and the coming of the kingdom of God. William Wrede produced a variation on Strauss's thesis in his book *The Messianic Secret in the Gospels* (1901). The early Church believed that Jesus was the Messiah, but to explain why he was not recognized as such during his lifetime, they invented the 'messianic secret', that Jesus had commanded them not to acknowledge this openly. According to Wrede, this is what is presented in Mark's Gospel, which was not historically reliable, but the story of Jesus creatively devised to illustrate Mark's theology.

Opposition to the whole project of writing biographies of Jesus was launched by Martin Kähler in his book *The So-called Historical Jesus and the Historic, Biblical Christ* (1892). It called in question the whole historical-critical method as a viable and legitimate way of trying to understand Jesus. But the final blow to the first 'quest' came from within the school of histor-ical-critical scholarship when Albert Schweitzer published a book in 1906, which in its English translation of 1910 was giv-en the title *The Quest of the Historical Jesus*. He saw three phases in the 'Quest'. In the first, stories of miracles and the super-natural were recognized as unhistorical myths, but Schleier-macher saw that Jesus' own religious experience was valuable. In the second stage, Baur and the Tübingen school dismissed the historicity of John and so the religious experience of Jesus was no longer accessible. In the third stage, Weiss had demol-ished the idea that Jesus was some kind of nineteenth-century social reformer. Rather, he preached a wild eschatology about the end of the world. Schweitzer accepted that view. Jesus had arranged his own crucifixion in an attempt to make God intervene to rescue him and bring in his kingdom, but he died disillusioned and despairing, exclaiming, 'My God! My God! Why have you forsaken me?' (see Matt. 27:46). All that was left was Jesus' ethics, living with love and respect for all living things, and Schweitzer went off to Africa (he was also a medical doctor) and ran a hospital for the rest of his life.

Schweitzer's book is held to have brought to an end what is now known as the 'first quest'. The Catholic scholar George Tyrrell summed up the failure of these Liberal Protestant writers and scholars. They had pursued a supposedly 'objective' method of Historiography but, before Weiss and Schweitzer at least, had in fact 'discovered' a Jesus who was made in their own image. They had read their own subjective concerns into Jesus. They had looked back through nineteen centuries and seen 'only the reflection of a Liberal Protestant face, seen at the bottom of a deep well.'[2]

Historiography and Hermeneutics

It seemed as if Historiography, the new science using the historical-critical method, was damaging to the Christian faith. This impression grew through the nineteenth century. The philosophy of Positivism initiated by Auguste Comte (1798–1857) argued for three stages in human development. The first lived with theological explanations for life's mysteries, the second with philosophical explanations, but now we were entering the scientific stage. He devised the new science of Sociology to offer scientific explanations for human life and society. Darwin's theory of evolution provoked a crisis for the deistic view of God the Creator by seeming to provide an alternative to the theory that God was the necessary designer of this intricate world. Deism began to slide into atheism or, at the very least, agnosticism.

In the field of Historiography, Leopold von Ranke (1795–1886) maintained that History should steer clear of theories: it simply recounted 'objective facts'. A more sophisticated view of Historiography and the interpretation of historical documents was proposed by two later thinkers. Wilhelm Dilthey (1833–1911) maintained that the human sciences could only understand human life and history through empathy. It is through

---

2. George Tyrrell, *Christianity at the Crossroads* (London: Longmans, Green, 1913), 44.

our own experience of life and world of meaning that we are able to read historical documents and enter in sympathetically to other human situations and cultures. This perspective was to lead to the development of Hermeneutics, the science of interpretation, but it also implied some kind of relativism.

Ernst Troeltsch (1865–1923) was the second thinker. He became a leading thinker in the 'History of Religions school'. He outlined three principles that, he maintained, must shape research into 'religion' and religious history. First was the principle of criticism. Since all religions now come under historical study and since historical argument only establishes probability and never absolute certainty, it is impossible to accept absolute claims or base religious belief on any single event. Second was the principle of analogy. While each historical event is unique, historians can only recognize facts that are analogous to their own experience of the world. (The influence of Hume can be seen here.) Third is the principle of correlation. All historical events must be correlated within the matrix of cause and effect in interconnected history, ruling out any recourse to supernatural explanations. Applied to Christianity, these principles were devastating. But Troeltsch seemed to be incapable of applying them consistently, judging monotheism to be 'superior' to polytheism. And it has been pointed out that these are not neutral or 'objective' principles as was often claimed. Rather, they were a formulation of metaphysical assumptions at least as dogmatic as the Christian beliefs Troeltsch rejected. It was in fact the dogma of Deism now inherited by atheism.

Given this apparent conflict between historical research and Christian belief, it is not surprising that a generation of theologians and biblical scholars after Schweitzer rejected the relevance of history for faith. Like Martin Kähler, they saw historical research as irrelevant. What mattered for Christian faith was the Christ of faith not the Jesus of history. Karl Barth (1886–1968) was part of that reaction, but a more extreme rejection of any role for history was that view of Rudolf Bultmann (1884–1976). He thought that the Gospels were so shaped by the theology of the early Church that they were not reliable historical accounts of the life of Jesus. That fitted with his Theology, however, for, as a Lutheran, Bultmann had his own interpretation of 'justification by faith', shaped by the philosophy of existentialism. Faith was not clinging to the dead old past but making the 'existential decision' to launch into a future life to live 'authentically' as Jesus had done. It was enough for Bultmann that Jesus had lived and died and brought us this Word from God. He had not literally, bodily, risen from the dead, but he lives in the experience and preaching of his apostles. The idea of a 'supernatural' God who intervened in the world was obsolete in the modern era. We could not live in a world with cars, radio, planes, and cinema and believe in a world of spirits and demons, heaven above and hell below. The New Testament had to be 'demythologized'.

The Second Quest

Bultmann's scepticism about the historical value of the New Testament was challenged by many of his contemporaries, including C.H. Dodd (1884–1973) of Manchester and Cambridge and Oscar Cullmann (1902-99) of Basel. But it was Bultmann's own doctoral students who launched what become known as the 'new quest' for the historical Jesus. Ernst Käsemann (1906-98) argued that one could trace a connection between the preaching of Jesus and the preaching of the early Church. Günter Bornkamm (1905-90) made that argument at length in his book, *Jesus of Nazareth*. Hans Conzelmann (1915-89), Ernst Fuchs (1903-83), and Gerhard Ebeling (1912–2001) took a similar line.

It is important for us to see, however, that this new quest was still based on the assumptions of Deism. It was not a neutral science despite its claim to be 'objective'. Its philosophical underpinnings were laid out in *The Historian and the Believer* (1969), a significant book by a professor at Stanford University, Van Harvey (1923–2021). He analyzed the logic of historical argument. The historian works from 'data' (or attested facts) to 'conclusions' that are reached according to 'warrants'. For example, given the *fact* that Jesus was crucified by the Romans, we can reach the *conclusion* that the Romans regarded him as dangerous via the *warrant* that the Romans crucified those they thought dangerous. Whereas a 'fact' is specific, a 'warrant' is a more general assumption or principle. But when it comes to the resurrection of Jesus, the problem for Christians is that the *datum* or *fact* that the tomb was empty cannot lead to the conclusion that Jesus rose from the dead because the only acceptable *warrant* is that dead men do not rise. Any other warrant would be contrary to Troeltsch's second and third principles. Harvey uses the word 'morality' here. It would be immoral to go against the modern view that we live in a world that is a closed system of cause and effect! That is the only 'scientific' view. Here quite clearly, Harvey's case is built on the dogma of Deism.

Harvey's conclusion is that he must rule out what he calls 'Hard Perspectivism', the idea that we must view Jesus from the perspective of his resurrection. He embraces instead what he calls 'Soft Perspectivism', the view taken by the scholars of the 'New Quest'. The resurrection of Jesus was not an additional historical fact, but simply a 'disclosure', the dawning of the right understanding of Jesus. It was simply the new confession that Jesus was the decisive witness to and awakener of faith. Although the scholars of the 'New Quest' took a more positive view of the historical value of the New Testament than Bultmann, in fact at the end of the day, they still shared his deistic assumptions.

The 'New Quest' seemed to run out of energy in the 1970s, but there was a revival of interest in the question of the 'historical' Jesus in the 1980s that has been labelled the 'Third Quest'. We shall reserve that term however for those scholars who took a much more positive view of the historicity of the Gospels. The scholars of the 'Jesus Seminar' in the 1980s and 1990s were actually carrying on the perspective of the 'New' or 'Second' Quest. Robert Funk initiated it in 1985 with the programme of voting on which sayings of Jesus could be regarded as authentic. The seminar represented as many views as it had participating scholars, but Burton L. Mack held a fairly typical viewpoint. The Gospel of Mark was, for him, largely fictional, and Jesus was probably a travelling Cynic philosopher who led a movement of social protest.

J.D. Crossan was another participant. He saw the Roman world as a 'brokered empire' with a network of master-slave and patron-client relationships that was breaking down in Palestine and leading eventually to revolution and the Roman destruction of Jerusalem in AD 70. Jesus was a travelling Cynic philosopher who was more accurately represented in the second-century *Gospel of Thomas* than in the four Gospels written in the first century. While Crossan may be right in his analysis of Roman society, his view of Jesus has generally been dismissed as a highly improbable scenario lacking in evidence. Altogether, with their concern with social issues and egalitarianism, some of the scholars of the 'Second Quest' were in danger once again of seeing their own faces at the bottom of the deep well of history.

Were the techniques of History, the historical-critical method, always bound to fail to account for Jesus? We shall examine the more positive conclusions of the 'Third Quest' in the next chapter.

TWO | The Jesus History Discovers

We are pursuing the question, 'Who is Jesus Christ?' So far, we have been examining the attempt of the modern study of history to answer that question. But as we have seen, that modern discipline emerged in a specific historical context, the culture of 'modern' Europe. The era of 'modernity' began in the Renaissance of the fifteenth and sixteenth centuries and reached its high point in the so-called Enlightenment of the eighteenth century. By then, the dominating outlook was that of Deism, which thought it was reasonable to believe in a transcendent god who had created the world but who did not intervene in its closed continuum of cause and effect. This was the background to the emergence of the nineteenth-century 'quest' for the 'historical' Jesus, revived in the 'New' or 'Second' Quest in the 1950s and continued in the work of the Jesus Seminar and scholars such as J.D. Crossan.

The Third Quest

Contemporary with the later scholars of the Jesus Seminar is a large group of scholars who take a more positive view of the historicity of the Gospels, and it is convenient to group them together under the heading of the 'Third Quest'. They are not all Christian believers but share common ground as scholars in their more positive historical conclusions. While not ignoring the wider context of Graeco-Roman society, they give more attention to the immediate context of the life of Jesus—Second Temple Judaism. This is the name given to Jewish religion and society as it developed from the building of the second temple in the sixth century BC until its destruction in AD 70. That context has been explored in the thorough researches of such scholars as E.P. Sanders (1937–2022) of Duke University and Martin Hengel (1926–2009) of Tübingen.

A number of historians may be included as contributing to this 'Third Quest'. The Jewish scholar Géza Vermes portrays Jesus as *hasid*, a charismatic holy man. Marcus Borg sees Jesus as a wisdom teacher who calls us to follow him in a life of prayer and compassion. He is closer to the scholars of the Second Quest in rejecting his resurrection and his divinity. Another group see Jesus as a prophet and reformer. E.P. Sanders dismisses the claim that he was a social reformer but affirms that he was a prophet proclaiming the coming kingdom of God. He accepts that his disciples 'saw' him (in some sense) after his crucifixion. His action in the temple was not so much a 'cleansing' as a prophetic action symbolizing its destruction, and he saw himself as God's eschatological viceroy. John P. Meier also sees Jesus as an eschatological prophet who spoke in riddles and so cannot be defined within any category. The conclusion of Crossan and the Jesus Seminar are 'largely fantasy' lacking historical evidence. Meier refuses to be dogmatic about the possibility of miracles, but he does not think that the historical-critical method can bring us all the way to faith.

Another group goes beyond classifying Jesus as a prophet to his claim to be the 'Messiah'. Ben Witherington shows that the term does not occur in the Hebrew Bible, that it was rare in Judaism, and that there was no agreed picture of who the Messiah would be or what he would do. Howard Marshall, James Dunn, and others argue that there was an expectation of a royal Messiah as a military leader but that Jesus redefined the role. Markus Bockmuehl and Marinus de Jonge agree that Jesus regarded himself as the Messiah, and de Jonge argues that Jesus saw himself as in some sense the 'Son of God'. Elisabeth Schüssler Fiorenza and Ben Witherington argue that Jesus identified himself with the figure of divine Wisdom.

At this point we must emphasize that these scholars are not expounding their theological beliefs. Some of them fully believe in Jesus as the incarnate Son of God, one with the Father from all eternity; others do not. But here they are engaging in the discipline of History and working out what may be established about Jesus according to the historical-critical method. The believers among them are accepting the limitations of the method in arguing to conclusions about historicity that even non-believers may accept, but they reserve their own position on whether we have to accept Troeltsch's three principles. In the end, as believers, they will not. But as scholars, they are accepting the limitations for the sake of argument to see what can be agreed as historically established.

Jesus and the God of Israel

So far, we have concentrated on 'Jesus' as a historical figure. But as many of the scholars of the 'Third Quest' have reminded us, to do this justice, we have to think of Jesus not only as a prophet but as 'the Christ', that is to say, the *Messiah* of Israel. We cannot understand Jesus except in the context of Israel, Israel's history, Israel's hopes, and Israel's God. To construct a historically accurate picture of Jesus, we have to understand the Jewish faith in which he was brought up. That means that we must begin with the Scriptures that he learned as a child and the practices that shaped his faith in the God of Israel.

The Hebrew Scriptures were vital to Israel's understanding of their God. The Torah—the five books of Moses—was of fundamental authority for all of Second Temple Judaism. Apart from the Sadducees, most groups accepted also the authority of the Former Prophets (which we call the Historical Books) and the Latter Prophets. The authority of Hebrew poetry and Wisdom literature was also widely accepted, although many other books such as the Wisdom of Solomon were also regarded as authoritative. The line had not yet been drawn around a definitive *canon* or list of authoritative books.

But although great prestige was given to the scribes and experts on the Torah, Second Temple Judaism did not have an abstract Systematic Theology. Rather, it was a practised faith, a *halakah* or way of life, in which daily life and conduct and practices were shaped by the Law—the Torah and the other Scriptures. If we ask therefore about the Jewish understanding of God, we can look at the great annual festivals commemorating the events of Israel's history in which their God had acted. The five most ancient festivals commemorated God's acts through Moses, and these pointed to the character of Israel's God.

First of all, in the Feast of Passover (*pesach*), usually in the month we call April, Israel celebrated the God of Redemption, 'the Lord' (they would not pronounce 'Yahweh', his holy name) who, in sheer grace and faithfulness to his covenant with the patriarchs, had delivered them from slavery in Egypt. This was the sovereign Lord who had revealed himself to Israel as their judge, king, warrior, and father. Secondly, seven weeks later, in the Feast of Pentecost (*shavu'ot*), Israel celebrated their God as the God of Covenant and Law. They recalled how at Sinai he had entered into solemn covenant, pledging himself to this people he had redeemed and issuing his sovereign law. Centred in the Ten Commandments, the law made clear his requirement that his people reflect his holiness.

Thirdly, four months later in the New Year festival (*rosh hashana*), Israel remembered among other things that their God was the Creator of the heavens and the earth. They also remembered that, of course, every Sabbath. Nine days later came the Day of Atonement (*yom kippur*), when they recognized their sinfulness over against the Holy God. The whole design and shape of the tabernacle, now reproduced in the second temple, emphasized the contrast between the holy and the profane, the pure and the defiled. The actions of the high priest that day enacted God's expiation of their sins and shortcomings and thus God's loving propitiation of his own fierce holiness. Five days later came the fifth Mosaic festival, Tabernacles (*succoth*), when Israel celebrated God as the God of Pilgrimage who had led them through the wilderness to the promised land and who would one day fulfil his promises to give Israel *shalom*.

They thus worshipped the God of Israel as the God of Redemption, the God of Covenant and Law, the Creator God, the Holy God, and the God of Pilgrimage. This was the God of Israel whom they celebrated in these great festivals. But it is important for us to realize that this was the God whom the boy known as *Yeshua* was brought up to love and obey. This was the God he trusted and whom he came to call 'Abba'. Nothing in all his teaching compromised any of this. Rather, he affirmed all this, even while correcting some of the misunderstandings of Jewish tradition. Nothing in his life, teaching, death, or resurrection contradicted this understanding of the God of Israel. On the contrary, those who follow Jesus must affirm the God of Israel whom he loved, honoured, and obeyed even to death.

The Jewish Worldview

There is more to say about Jesus as the Christ, the Messiah of Israel, and no one has done more to help us see this than the New Testament scholar N.T. Wright. Tom Wright engaged for decades in a massive work of scholarship with six volumes under the general title of *Christian Origins and the Question of God*. The first two volumes are directly relevant to the question of the 'quest' for the 'historical' Jesus.[1] Wright is alert to literary questions about the Bible as narrative and to the theological implications of his research, but the heart of his thinking is a sophisticated understanding of the methodology of the historian.

He analyses the worldview of the Jews of Jesus' day by examining the four relevant symbols of their faith—the temple, the land, the Torah, and their racial identity. These were integral to their *halakha*—way of life. But these reveal that their monotheism was not a philosophical monotheism like that of the Greek philosophers, but the belief that the Creator of heaven and earth had entered into covenant with them and was present in their temple. That posed a theological problem: Why then had they been subjugated for centuries to exile and subjugation to the great powers? And why had it not yet come to an end with the restoration of sovereignty ('the kingdom') to Israel at the 'Day of the Lord'? That was Israel's great hope.

Wright argues that it is only against this background that we can understand the thinking and intentions of Jesus. Historians face the challenge of explaining how the followers of this crucified man had developed by AD 110 into a large and vigorous international movement. They are therefore

---

1. These are *The New Testament and the People of God* (London: SPCK, 1992) and *Jesus and the Victory of God* (London: SPCK, 1996).

faced with the questions of how he fits into Judaism, what his aims were, why he died, and how and why the Church began. Wright accepts the consensus across the scholars of the 'Third Quest' that Jesus thought of himself as a prophet. He did not teach timeless truths or a new spirituality or issue a call to existential decision but was announcing the reign of Israel's God, the 'kingdom'. But Jesus gave this familiar hope a new twist. His parables were subversive and therefore deliberately cryptic. When he spoke of the kingdom of God, he was invoking a familiar storyline, but subverting the usual conclusion. He was summoning his followers to be Israel in a new way as he launched the decisive battle against the real enemy, the satan (adversary).

The action of Israel's God was to be seen in the welcome Jesus gave to 'sinners'. The prophets had seen the exile as God's punishment for Israel's sin, but the forgiveness of sin (that is, the true return from exile) was not through the sacrifices of the temple or allegiance to the Torah, but through allegiance to Jesus. He believed that Israel's story was heading for a great disaster but that those who followed him would be delivered and vindicated. This, rather than a prophecy of a second coming, was the meaning of his warnings in Mark 13.

The Mindset of Jesus

Wright is trying to understand the mindset of Jesus in fully human terms, and Christians cannot object to that without falling into the heresy of Apollinarianism (that Jesus did not have a human mind). He agrees with those scholars of the Third Quest who argue that Jesus regarded himself as the Messiah. But we must understand that in Judaism the messianic title 'Son of God' did not carry the implication of deity. The evidence of his messianic claim was first his 'triumphal entry' into Jerusalem, then his action in the temple claiming royal authority over it, the series of 'six royal riddles' in his teaching in the temple, and notably the parable of the vineyard. He was arrested and tried as a dangerous political nuisance who might bring down the wrath of Rome on the Jewish establishment.

But why did he intend to die? Wright begins with the key symbol of the Last Supper. His actions with the bread and cup at this Passover meal were prophetic acts indicating (along with his temple action) that he was replacing the temple system. In prophetic style, he identified the bread with his own body and the wine with his blood and used Passover language to speak of sacrifice and covenant. He was about to die, but his death would bring about the renewal of the covenant. This was the climactic moment to which the whole story of Israel was pointing.

What did Jesus think would happen next? Wright concludes that he expected some kind of battle, not against the occupying forces, but against 'the satan'. And he would fight this by himself turning the other cheek, going the second mile, loving his enemies, and praying for his persecutors. Wright comes to this conclusion:

> I propose, then, that we can credibly reconstruct a mindset in which a first-century Jew could come to believe that YHWH would act through the sufferings of a particular individual in whom Israel's sufferings were focused; that this suffering would carry redemptive significance; *and that this individual would be himself.* And I propose that we can plausibly suggest that this was the mindset of Jesus himself.[2]

Scholars like Marcus Borg take a different view, and even some Evangelical scholars demur over Wright's interpretation of Mark 13, but it is widely agreed that, using the historical-critical method, Wright has established a strong case for the substantial historicity of the portrayal of Jesus in the Gospels. But the crunch comes when we turn to the historicity of the resurrection.

History and the Resurrection

It is when we come to the final episodes in the Gospel narrative that the true challenge comes to the deist rejection of God's direct action in his world. Here, as we have seen, deists share the same view as atheists and agnostics that 'miracles' do not happen. They share the secular perspective of moder-

---

2. Wright, *Jesus and the Victory of God*, 593.

nity. It is one thing for them to look for other explanations for the various miracle stories in the Gospels, but when it comes to the resurrection of Jesus, we are thinking of one unparalleled and unprecedented miracle that is pivotal for the whole Christian faith. Do modern secular presuppositions rule it out as unhistorical? Or is it rather that the resurrection of Jesus presents the greatest challenge to modern secularism and its role in the historical-critical method?

In the twentieth century, Karl Barth and Rudolf Bultmann shared the view of Martin Kähler that historical research was irrelevant. But there was a major difference between them. Barth believed in the bodily resurrection of Jesus, but he thought that the historical-critical method was irrelevant to faith. Only by the Holy Spirit could we come to believe in the risen Lord. Bultmann did not believe in the bodily resurrection of Jesus. Such a belief belonged to a past, unscientific age. But what mattered for him was that the disciples came to believe that Jesus had brought the Word of God, the Gospel that we are justified by faith. It was that Gospel which released us to live 'authentically', not clinging to the dead old past, but making the existential decision to be open to God's future. That was what mattered.

Pannenberg and Wright

Wolfhart Pannenberg (1928–2014) disagreed with them both and gave much greater weight to the historical-critical method as the way to faith.[3] For Pannenberg, God's revelation was not merely the Bible, nor even the salvation history it recounted, but comprised the whole of world history. The influence of Hegel can be seen here: God's revelation would be complete at the end of world history. But for Pannenberg, the 'End' had appeared in advance in Jesus Christ, God Incarnate, and that was revealed in his resurrection, an event that could be proved by historical research. The historical-critical method could bring us to faith.

3. See Wolfhart Pannenberg, *Basic Questions in Theology*, vol. 1 (London: SCM, 1970).

Significant here was Pannenberg's critique of Troeltsch's three principles of historical method. He attacked particularly his third principle, the principle of analogy, that we must assume that all events are analogous to events we ourselves have experienced. This dictated that we had to assume a closed continuum of cause and effect, but Pannenberg attacked this as dependent on a metaphysical materialism. In other words, it was not the neutral position it pretended to be, hiding under the guise of 'modern science'. It was rather captive to secularist, materialist dogma. It was 'scientism' rather than science. It was bound by the dogma of Historicism. Once that was dismissed, examining the historical evidence—the empty tomb and the appearances to the apostles—made it clear that the conclusion that Jesus had risen from the dead was eminently reasonable. On the basis of the evidence and without these dogmatic presuppositions, there was no other credible explanation.

N.T. Wright tackles the issues in the third volume of his series, *The Resurrection of the Son of God*.[4] Wright, along with Pannenberg, rejects the view that this is irrelevant to faith. He goes on to demonstrate that it is broadly true (though it was not universal) that Jews believed in bodily resurrection, while Greeks, under the influence of Plato, believed in the immortality of the soul. It was this Jewish belief that the apostle Paul held, but it had been modified when he had encountered the risen Lord. Now he declared that Jesus had *already* been raised from the dead in anticipation of the last general resurrection of all. Wright particularly examines 1 Corinthians 15 to refute the idea that by the phrase 'a spiritual body' Paul meant a non-material body. Rather, the chapter confirms that Paul believed that Jesus had risen bodily from the grave. Wright finds that this is confirmed by examining 2 Corinthians 4:7–5:10 and the resurrection narratives in the Gospels.

Wright's claim is that it is beyond all reasonable doubt that the early Church truly believed and intended to teach that Jesus was raised from the dead in a bodily resurrection

---

4. N.T. Wright, *The Resurrection of the Son of God*, vol. 3 of *Christian Origins and the Question of God* (London: SPCK, 2003).

that transformed his crucified body into what Wright calls a 'transphysical' body. The two pieces of evidence, the empty tomb and his appearances to the apostles, provided *sufficient* evidence to make this a reasonable belief. But more than that, the two pieces of evidence are *necessary* to that belief. It could not have arisen without both of them. The conclusion follows for us as historians today that the tomb must have been empty. The belief in his resurrection could not have arisen without that. And equally, the apostles must have been convinced that they had met him. Wright concludes, 'I regard this conclusion as coming in the same sort of category, of historical probability so high as to be virtually certain, as the death of Augustus in AD 14 or the fall of Jerusalem in AD 70.'[5]

It is the historical evidence for the resurrection of Jesus that brings to a head the question of the historical-critical method. What are we to make of the claim that the resurrection of Jesus is historically established fact? And what are the implications of claiming that the historical-critical method can establish this fact?

Can History Accept Miracles?

We begin with the second question: Can History as an academic discipline, or the scientific disciplines in general, accept miracles? But the question is much larger than that. To make the question merely the question of miracles and to define a miracle as a breaking of the 'laws of nature' is to submit to the dogma of secularism or 'Naturalism'. It is the bias or prejudice that only some form of secularism, either deistic or atheistic, can be regarded as intellectually or academically acceptable. Certainly in the world of Western academia today, that is the ruling 'plausibility structure'. But over against that, we have millennia of theism—Jewish, Christian, and Islamic—three ancient traditions very much alive and spreading in the world today. All of the great minds and cultural wealth of those great traditions of theism cannot be simply dismissed with an arrogant wave of the hand. Moreover, it has been a

---

5. Wright, *Resurrection*, 710.

feature of the theistic perspective that God's action in the world is *hidden*. For Christian belief in particular, we are still living in 'this present evil age', the era or *saeculum* when the kingdom of God has not yet come in glory and power. That means that we cannot dispense with a 'secular' (as distinct from 'secularist') viewpoint.

It is important therefore to distinguish here between a *methodological* secularism and a *metaphysical* secularism. Christians can live with the former. Granted that God is the Supreme Mystery and that the action of God in the world is generally *hidden*, we cannot pronounce definitively on acts of God in our writing of world history in general. The Christian faith does not give definitive pronouncements on how God was active in the history of Europe or Africa, Asia, or the Americas. Nor does it give definitive pronouncements about acts of God in any other of the human or natural sciences. In all of these, Christians accept the *methodological secularism*. These are part of the 'rules of the game', the accepted methodology of the arts and sciences. We may believe as Christians that God in his sovereignty was active in, for example, the defeat of the monstrous Nazi tyranny, but we do not bring that into our writing of secular history—the history of this *saeculum*.

'Secularism' wants to extend this *methodological* rule into a *metaphysical* one. There is no Creator God, and everything must be accounted for within a closed continuum of cause and effect. But that is not a neutral position. It is a declaration of faith. It is the faith or conviction of Secular Humanism, expressed in the dogma that the material universe is itself the Ultimate Reality ('Naturalism') and that the good of the human race is the Ultimate Value. These two are in fact in conflict with each other so that this Humanist faith is incoherent. The conclusion that follows from *metaphysical* Naturalism is that sentient, intelligent, personal life is one great accident with no ultimate value. Ethics is a mirage or at best social convention, and eventually the human race will perish when catastrophe finally overtakes the planet and indeed the universe itself.

The resurrection of Jesus challenges us to consider another possibility. It is that the Creator God, although the Supreme

Mystery hidden and indeed alienated from his estranged and defiled creatures, has in fact been working with a redemptive purpose through the long centuries of human evil. His largely hidden action in the history of Israel has come to its climax in the resurrection of Jesus. Jesus therefore has to be recognized as God Incarnate, God himself in human form, the Messiah in whom the hidden God is revealed and vindicated.

But if we are to embrace this good news, what would that imply for our understanding of the discipline of History, not to mention all the other human and natural sciences? Would we have to abandon the historical-critical method or any attempt at critical history? Would we have to abandon all this-worldly secular sciences? Would we have to make theology 'queen of the sciences' in the sense that all our intellectual endeavour and academic disciplines must be deduced from the text of the Bible? In short, do we have to be fundamentalists in order to be Christians? Specifically, does this require us to abandon the historical-critical method when it comes to faith?

History and Faith

Keeping specifically to this question of history and faith, we can identify several schools of thought among scholars and theologians within the Christian tradition. There is, first of all, the tradition we may label 'Liberal' or, more accurately, 'modernist'. For them, 'modern' thought since the Enlightenment is definitive. This is the tradition of the 'quest' for the 'historical' Jesus that we have traced from Schleiermacher and Hegel down through Strauss and Baur. We saw it continuing in Bultmann's disciples in what we now call the 'Second Quest', down to the Jesus Seminar and John Dominic Crossan. The methodology of this tradition was spelled out by Troeltsch and later by Van Harvey. It dismisses the historicity of the resurrection and often sits loose to the deity of Christ. Over against this, we can identify a tradition that accepts the historicity of the bodily resurrection of Jesus and confesses him as Lord and God. But within this broad school of Christian orthodoxy, we may identify two schools of thought often considered to be in tension.

First, there are those who champion the value of historical research into the life of Jesus. The leading figures (despite real differences between them) we have identified as Oscar Cullmann, Wolfhart Pannenberg, and N.T. Wright. Cullmann championed the perspective of 'salvation history' in opposition to Bultmann in a way endorsed by the American Biblical Theology movement. Pannenberg criticized the notion of 'salvation history' and employed the somewhat Hegelian notion that it was the whole of world history that would reveal God at 'the End'. The 'End' or 'Eschaton' had come early however and was present in Jesus, whose resurrection could be established as fact by the historical-critical method. Pannenberg claimed that this established the deity of Christ 'from below', but he had in fact already argued from the superiority of apocalyptic Judaism and its belief in resurrection over modern secularism. Whereas Pannenberg argued this case as a systematic theologian, N.T. Wright argues essentially as a historian that there is no explanation for the historical phenomenon of the rise of the Christian Church other than the resurrection of her Lord.

The other school of thought is rather more negative about the role of the historical-critical method. This way of thinking may be associated with Martin Kähler, Karl Barth, and Hans Frei, with roots back in Søren Kierkegaard. Kähler's total rejection of historical research may be an overreaction, but he was fundamentally right that it is the preached Christ, proclaimed in the New Testament Gospel, which is the only true interpretation of who Jesus was and is. The same may be said for Barth. Like Kähler, he believed in the bodily resurrection of Jesus but saw the historical-critical method as a dead end. To adopt the methodology espoused by Troeltsch is to restrict our understanding of history to the human and cultural and to rule out any possibility of an act of God from the start. In complete opposition to that, Barth emphasized that it was not possible to come to faith in Jesus Christ at the end of a line of historical reasoning. It was only possible when we are enlightened by the Holy Spirit. Faith is a mystery held within the action of the Holy Trinity. Hans Frei similarly dismissed historical-critical research. We are not concerned with the events 'behind the text' but with the world we discover 'in the text'.

The Resurrection: History and Eschatology

What are we to make of these two schools of thought within Christian orthodoxy, both accepting the bodily resurrection of Jesus from the dead? It has been suggested that the real difference between them is that the first regards the resurrection of Jesus as a *historical* event, open to historical research, whereas the second regards it as an *eschatological* event of the age to come not open to investigation within this *saeculum*, 'this present evil age'. But perhaps the resolution of the debate is to be found in the observation that it is *both*. The resurrection of Jesus is *both* an event of history *and* the intrusion of 'the age to come', the kingdom of God, into our fallen age. T.F. Torrance sums up the point:

> In other words, we can interpret the resurrection only if we interpret it theologically as well as historically. It will not do however, to interpret it merely 'theologically' as if it could be done apart from history, for that would mythologize and docetize it, and then we would have nothing to interpret. Nor can we interpret it merely 'historically' in the sense that we interpret other historical events in human history, only by reference to human agency and natural processes, for that would be tantamount to insisting that all we have here is an ordinary historical happening, and so to rejecting from the start the claim that the Agent is the Son of God.[6]

In the light of this analysis then it is possible for us to see that these two schools of thought are complementary rather than contradictory. They agree that the problem lies with the methodology of History as it emerged out of the Enlightenment and was analyzed by Troeltsch. The Kähler school apparently accepts the secular methodology of History but argues that it simply cannot cope with God's eschatological action in Jesus. The other school is more optimistic about what the discipline of History can accept. It can accept that it is doctrinaire secularism to reject on principle that God cannot act in the

---

6. T.F. Torrance, *Space, Time and Resurrection* (Edinburgh: Handsel Press, 1976), 94. Docetism was the heresy that Christ was God but not human.

world. That does not mean that it will accept any miraculous tale or be open to superstition, but where a strong case can be made, it is not bound to the dogma of Deism or atheism or secularism. It cannot rule out God's action in the world where the evidence is compelling.

The complementarity between the two views can therefore be expressed paradoxically. The Christian faith could be disproved by History, but History cannot prove the faith. Faith is subject to History in the sense that, in the unlikely event that history disproved the life, death, and resurrection of Jesus, the Christian faith would fall. It is in principle falsifiable and therefore is not some esoteric religion but makes truth claims in the space-time world. Without that, it would be reduced to some kind of spiritual myth or existentialism. But on the other hand, History cannot prove the faith. The proof of the historicity of Jesus of Nazareth is beyond reasonable doubt. But the fact that there is no other tenable historical explanation for his resurrection does not provide a knock-down Cartesian argument that Christianity is true. There is no rationalistic ladder of proof by which we can mount to heaven. Historical research only brings us to the threshold. But it does bring us to that threshold.

On the Threshold of Faith

We are faced with the question of what happened on Easter morning and the impossibility of explaining as historians the rise of the Christian Church and the writing of the New Testament documents unless we accept as compelling the evidence that Jesus actually rose from the dead leaving the tomb empty and appeared to witnesses. To describe this conclusion as 'compelling' is not to say, of course, that it cannot be rejected. Even though the evidence is compelling, we can reject it, not because we have a superior historical explanation (there is none), but simply on ideological grounds. If we are determined to do so, we may take our stance on the dogma of 'Naturalism' or secularism, namely, that reality is restricted to the physical space-time universe we apprehend through our five senses. Or we may try to survive in the halfway house of

Deism, imagining our own version of a transcendent god, but one who is either shut out of his creation or indifferent to it.

If we are truly agnostic however, we will be genuinely open-minded to the hidden Mystery of the living God. The historic faith of Israel, reaching its culmination in the life, preaching, character, claims, and death of Jesus of Nazareth, and the strong historical evidence for his resurrection, will lead us to ask ourselves seriously whether we are genuinely open to all of this. The claim is that this is the self-revelation of the God who is not accessible to our five senses within our universe, but who is hidden from us 'in light unapproachable' (1 Tim. 6:16, ASV).

Of course such a possibility questions us to the very roots of our being. If this mysterious God was truly active in the history of Israel, and if his revealing of himself truly came to its culmination in Jesus of Nazareth, then the unique stature of the man Jesus cuts the ground from under our feet. We can no longer pretend to be neutral, objective Enlightenment philosophers sitting in judgment on the question of God. We are forced to recognize that in Jesus as the culmination and fulfilment of the faith of Israel, we are revealed by contrast to be not only moral weaklings but selfish, proud, guilty sinners.

The breathtaking audacity of the claim of Jesus in Mark 13:31, that heaven and earth may pass away, but that his words will never pass away, confronts us with the challenge of such a radical repentance and re-orientation of all our thinking and assumptions that we are called to fall at his feet and confess him to be Lord and God.

We cross that threshold only by a complete transformation of our whole outlook, a repentance, a conversion, a paradigm shift, brought about as the gift of God the Holy Spirit so that we can recognize the truth—Jesus Christ as Lord.

PART I
Jesus Christ in Scripture and Tradition

THREE

Jesus Revealed in the Gospel

Once we have knelt before the risen Lord like Thomas and confessed 'My Lord and my God!' (John 20:28), the way is open to know him and express that knowledge. At this point, we realize that he is not merely a historical figure but our contemporary. We have no access to historical figures of the past except by the historical-critical method. But once we realize that Jesus is risen from the dead and is alive today in the power of his Holy Spirit, then we can truly come to know him. Only then can we explore who he is and express and formulate that knowledge. This is not only an academic but a personal knowledge. As the Church, we express that knowledge together in the teaching we call 'Christology', the doctrine of the Person of Christ. It is the confession of our faith in him.

No doubt, unbelievers may consider the Christian doctrine of Christ, trace its history, and examine its logic, but for them that is merely an intellectual game. For those of us who believe in Jesus, this is the expression of our faith in the One we have come to know. He is the One in whom we trust through life and in death. What shall we say about him? How shall we distinguish between the truth about him and the distortions and lies?

At this point, to begin to articulate our knowledge of who he is we have to begin with the witnesses he has appointed—the apostles. At their heart stand the Twelve, but they were part of a wider group—all that generation who were witnesses to his life and teaching, his death and resurrection. Matthias had to be in this wider group in order to be admitted to the Twelve (Acts 1:21-22). Paul and Barnabas were among them (14:14), as were many others such as Andronicus and

Junias, possibly husband and wife (Rom. 16:7). Paul refers at one point to five hundred of them (1 Cor. 15:6). They were that generation who witnessed his life, death, and resurrection and whose testimony was included in the four Gospels. How did the apostles come to confess the deity of Christ?

Jews and the Deity of Christ

Over the last century, scholars have been examining this and asking, How did the New Testament accounts of Jesus take shape? The specific question was, How could these Jews come to confess that Jesus Christ was 'Lord'? How could these fiercely monotheistic members of Judaism come to make the so apparently blasphemous statement that this man was God? After two thousand years of Christian history, the enormity of this may not strike us. But how was this possible? This was another 'quest', not into the historicity of Jesus himself, but rather into the history of the early Church. And once again, the historical-critical method was employed to answer the question of how belief in the deity of Christ developed.

Early in the twentieth century, scholars of what was known as the 'History of Religions School' thought that the belief in the deity of Christ must necessarily have developed slowly in a very long process. This view was expressed with impressive scholarship in *Kyrios Christos* (1913), a work by the German scholar Wilhelm Bousset (1865–1920). He thought that passionately monotheistic Jews could not possibly have originated this belief in the deity of Christ. Rather, it must have developed late in the first century among Greek-speaking gentiles in Graeco-Roman culture, which had a custom of 'deifying' great men such as Caesar. It became the standard view that the New Testament had developed slowly over decades. Rudolf Bultmann originated the idea that the stories about Jesus in the Gospels had been reshaped during this long oral phase as they were told and retold in various Christian 'communities'. For Bultmann, that meant that they had little historical value but were 'redacted' during this period of 'oral transmission' to meet the needs of these later generations. 'Form criticism' and 'redaction criticism' were developed to show how this had been done.

In the middle of the twentieth century, several scholars saw the importance of the titles given to Jesus in the New Testament. Oscar Cullmann of Basel argued that the question, 'Who is Jesus?' was always linked in the New Testament with the question of his role or function.[1] This was always expressed in titles: 'Prophet, High Priest, Mediator, Servant of God, Lamb of God, Messiah, Son of David, Son of Man, Judge, Holy One of God, Lord, Saviour, King, Logos, Son of God.'[2] Other scholars, such as Ferdinand Hahn of Kiel and R.H. Fuller of Union Seminary, New York, thought that they could place the development of these titles historically. Some titles originated in the original 'community' of Palestinian Jews who were the first Christians, others developed in the next stage among those of the Greek-speaking Jewish 'community', and others eventually came about among Greek Christians. Only at this third stage did titles develop that asserted Christ's deity. This was in line with Bousset's theory, but Martin Hengel and E.P. Sanders demolished the assumption that these three 'communities' formed discrete groups. The theory was far too tidy and far too dependent on Bousset.

James Dunn of Durham University saw that the titles could not be considered in isolation but that the development of New Testament Christology had to be seen as a whole. He concentrated on the *kerygma*, the preached Gospel of the apostles, and argued that while it took many forms, it had a common heart: 'the unity between the exalted Christ and Jesus of Nazareth, the crucified one who is also the risen one.'[3] Dunn went on to argue that this earliest proclamation of the apostles developed later with the emergence of the belief that this one, who was crucified and rose again, was the incarnation of the Wisdom of the Word of God.[4]

---

1. Oscar Cullmann, *The Christology of the New Testament* (London: SCM, 1959).

2. Cullmann, 8.

3. James D.G. Dunn, *Unity and Diversity in the New Testament: An Inquiry into the Character of Earliest Christianity* (London: SCM, 1977), 203.

4. James D.G. Dunn, *Christology in the Making: An Inquiry into the Origins of the Doctrine of the Incarnation* (London: SCM, 1980).

The Worship of Jesus

Something of a revolution in the study of New Testament Christology has taken place since. Larry Hurtado (1943–2019) of the University of Edinburgh argued that to understand the development behind the Christology of the New Testament, we must note the evidence of devotion to Christ that appeared at the very earliest stage of development. In a passage in 1 Corinthians, one of the earliest books of the New Testament, written within twenty years of the crucifixion, Paul rewrites the *Shema*, the ancient proclamation from Deuteronomy 6 of Jewish monotheism. He *includes* the Lord Jesus Christ *within* the one God we are to worship (1 Cor. 8:5-6).[5] Hurtado marshals the evidence to show that 'within the first two decades of Christianity, Jewish Christians gathered in Jesus' name for worship, prayed to him and sang hymns to him . . . appropriated to him titles and Old Testament passages referring to God.'[6]

Hurtado agreed with Bousset that historians are competent to determine when the confession of the deity of Christ arose. But he differed completely in his conclusion. If he is right, all the developments from Bousset through Bultmann have to be rethought. Not all New Testament scholars would agree, but what we can say is that there is now a strong case made by the highest scholarship that, from the resurrection, Christians worshipped Jesus as 'Lord', identifying him with the God of Israel.

Further strength is given to Hurtado's case by the work of Richard Bauckham of St. Andrews. Bauckham has drawn attention to the importance in ancient historiography of first-hand witnesses to historic events. Contrary to the notion of the long development of the stories of the Gospels through anonymous 'communities', there is every reason to think that the three Synoptic Gospels embody the testimony of eyewit-

---

5. Larry Hurtado, *One God, One Lord: Early Christian Devotion and Ancient Christian Monotheism* (Minneapolis: Augsburg Fortress, 1988), 1.

6. Larry Hurtado, *Lord Jesus Christ: Devotion to Jesus in Earliest Christianity* (Grand Rapids: Eerdmans, 2003), 11.

nesses.[7] There is a strong case, too, that John's Gospel was written by someone who was himself an eyewitness.[8]

With renewed confidence in the four Gospels, we may turn to them and the other New Testament books to find the Gospel that the apostles preached, for it is by their witness that we come to know and recognize who Jesus is. It is in and through their narrative of the Gospel that we may come to know him.

Narrative and Identity

Hans Frei (1922-88) helps us to understand how this works. In his book *The Identity of Jesus Christ* (1975), Frei lays aside the historical question, the reality and the events *behind the text*, to concentrate on what is *in the text*. In the end, that is Frei's weakness, since in a faith centred on the Incarnate God, we ultimately cannot lay aside that question. But as an interim step, it is very helpful. It helps us to focus on the text itself—the *narrative*—and the way in which it conveys the *identity* of its primary character. Frei proposes two questions to put to the text or narrative in order to come to know the characters within it.

The first question, 'What is he like?' probes the way in which a person's actions illuminate and even *constitute* his or her character. A person is what she *does* intentionally. Intention and actions can be distinguished, but their unity is an irreversible movement from one to the other. The second question, 'Who is he?' is harder, since it may not be clear to what the word 'he' refers. The subject or 'self' is elusive, and yet there is a unity between the self and its *manifestations* in its 'word' and in its 'body'. A person is revealed to us in his words and his bodily actions.

Applying this to the narrative of the New Testament, and asking of Jesus, 'What is he like?' Frei sees the defining characteristic is his obedience to God and yet his intentional action

---

7. Richard Bauckham, *Jesus and the Eyewitnesses: The Gospels as Eyewitness Testimony* (Grand Rapids: Eerdmans, 2006).

8. Richard Bauckham, *The Testimony of the Beloved Disciple* (Grand Rapids: Baker, 2007).

can always be distinguished from the intentional actions of God. The second question, 'Who is he?' focuses our attention on the continuity of his identity through the story.

Richard Bauckham employs the concept of *identity* in his book *God Crucified*.[9] The identity of God is revealed in the narrative of the Old Testament. Some of his identifying features reveal him as the God of Israel, Yahweh; others, as the Lord of all the earth, the Creator. In the intertestamental literature, those Jewish books written between the Testaments, intermediary figures appear—God's Word and Wisdom, principal angels and exalted patriarchs. Some scholars have seen these as providing the steps in the development of belief in the deity of Christ. But according to Bauckham, this is the exact opposite of the truth. Hellenism had a rising scale of deity, but Judaism could not tolerate semi-divine figures.

Right from the beginning of the Church therefore, Jesus was included within the divine identity of the God of Israel. Paul's rewriting of the *Shema* in 1 Corinthians 8:5-6 redefines monotheism as Christological monotheism. The unique identity of the one God consists of one God, the Father, and one Lord, his Messiah. Bauckham concludes: 'A higher Christology than Paul already expresses in 1 Corinthians 8:6 is scarcely possible.'[10] Given then that the apostles are trustworthy witnesses, what do they say of Jesus? What is their narrative, the story that they tell about him?

The One-in-Two Gospel of Jesus

The canonical order of the New Testament books seems to tell the story in *chronological* order—the life, death, and resurrection of Jesus in the four Gospels, followed by the narrative of the early Church in the book of Acts and the apostles' letters to the churches. But there is another order—the order in which these books were written. Here, the epistles come first as the older documents and the four Gospels later. Of

---

9. Richard Bauckham, *God Crucified: Monotheism and Christology in the New Testament* (Carlisle, UK: Paternoster, 1998). This is the published version of the Didsbury Lectures, given at Nazarene Theological College, Manchester.

10. Bauckham, 40.

course, the life and teaching of Jesus that the Gospels narrate came before the writing of the epistles.

In chronological order of events then, what came first was the teaching of Jesus. What is striking about the accounts of this in the Gospels, written *after* the epistles, is how little they incorporate the later apostolic teaching. In other words, they appear to reflect the teaching of Jesus accurately.[11] The background was the eschatological hope of the Jews that at the end of this evil age, God would re-establish his kingdom, the kingdom of Israel. Against that background, we see the teaching of Jesus that 'the kingdom of God is at hand' (Mark 1:15). As scholars long ago concluded, this is the paradoxical proclamation that the kingdom of God is both 'already' but 'not yet'. Jesus' exorcisms demonstrate that in Jesus the kingdom is *already* present (Luke 11:20), and yet Jesus has just taught his disciples to pray that the kingdom may come (v. 2). This is Jesus' Gospel of the kingdom, and it has what we shall call the paradoxical 'one-in-two' shape.

The One-in-Two Gospel of the Apostles

It is out of this that the Gospel of the apostles developed. We can see its basic shape in the speeches in the book of Acts. In Peter's first speech on the day of Pentecost, he points to Joel's prophecy of the pouring out of the Spirit in 'the last days' (Acts 2:17) but then goes straight to proclaim Jesus. 'God has made him both Lord and Christ, this Jesus whom you crucified' (v. 36). Crucifixion and resurrection are the one-in-two shape of the apostolic Gospel. Peter's speech after the healing of the lame man has the same one-in-two structure (3:14-15), as does his speech before the Sanhedrin (4:10). When he preaches to the gentiles, we find it again: 'They put him to death by hanging him on a tree; but God raised him on the third day' (10:39-40; see vv. 38-42). This Gospel of Christ is

11. Markus Bockmuehl comments on how *little* the Gospels reflect the later Hellenistic culture of the young churches. See Bockmuehl, 'God's Life as a Jew: Remembering the Son of God as Son of David', in *Seeking the Identity of Jesus: A Pilgrimage*, ed. B. Gaventa and R. Hays (Grand Rapids: Eerdmans, 2008), 71.

the source of salvation, which is to be found in him alone and 'in no one else' (4:12).

The one-in-two structure of Jesus' proclamation of the already-not-yet kingdom has now become the one-in-two structure of the apostolic Gospel—crucifixion and resurrection. The one who lived and suffered and died in the *not-yet* age of evil and death is now *already* in the kingdom of resurrection life. His one-in-two narrative of the Gospel of the kingdom is now embodied in the one-in-two narrative of cross and resurrection. And it is in this narrative that we learn his *identity*. Whereas his earthly life all the way to death reveals his true *humanity*, his exaltation in resurrection and ascension calls forth the confession that he is not only 'Christ', the Messiah, but he is 'Lord'. From Peter's speech on the day of Pentecost onward, the apostles quote Psalm 110, the psalm to which Jesus himself had drawn attention (Mark 12:35-37): 'The LORD says to my lord: "Sit at my right hand, till I make your enemies your footstool"' (Ps. 110:1). The apostles took this to mean that Jesus was exalted to the very throne of God. The one-in-two *narrative* of the Gospel thus gives us the *identity* of the one-in-two Saviour—fully human and fully God.

It is this same Gospel we find in the preaching of Paul. It is reckoned that the conversion of Paul came within two years of the crucifixion and resurrection.[12] Around twenty years later, he wrote a letter to the church in Corinth in which he summarized the Gospel he had preached to them on his first visit a few years earlier:

> Christ died for our sins in accordance with the scriptures, and that he was buried, and that he was raised on the third day in accordance with the scriptures, and that he appeared to Cephas, then to the twelve. (1 Cor. 15:3*b*-5, NRSV)

Here again in the earliest documentary evidence we have is the one-in-two shape of the narrative, crucifixion and resurrection, with its implications for salvation. The one-in-two structure is evident, too, a few years later when Paul penned

---

12. See Hurtado, *Lord Jesus Christ*, 83.

his great letter to the Roman Christians by summarizing the Gospel of God:

> . . . the gospel concerning his Son, who was descended from David according to the flesh and was declared to be Son of God with power according to the spirit of holiness by resurrection from the dead, Jesus Christ our Lord . . . (Rom. 1:3-4, NRSV)

Paul quotes this to the Romans as the Gospel held in common by all the apostles and all the churches. As Terence Donaldson has put it, 'Before there were the Gospels, there was the Gospel.'[13] It was this Gospel, held in common by the apostles, which preceded all the epistles and Gospels, which was at the root and origin of them all.

Paul not only quotes the Gospel but also draws out its implications in his epistles. And among the developments that come very early indeed is the implication that if Jesus Christ is 'Lord', that is, identified by his exaltation with the God of Israel, then we must confess that he has been so from all eternity. That implies that he has *become* human for us. Although Paul does not use the word, the 'Incarnation' is therefore clear in Paul's teaching, clearly expressed in a set of 'hymns' that he composed himself or quotes.

The Christological Hymns

The Christological 'hymn' in Philippians 2 is clearly the narrative of the Gospel, but the pattern of crucifixion and resurrection is extended into a full sweep of descent and ascent. It begins with the eternal pre-existence of the one already named as 'Christ Jesus' (v. 5). He existed (*hyparxōn*) in the form (*morphē*) of God but emptied (*ekenōsen*) himself, taking the form (*morphē*) of a slave. And being found in human shape (*schēmati*), he humbled himself by being obedient unto death, even death on a cross. God then becomes the subject of the following verbs. God highly exalted (*hyperypsōsen*) him, giving him the divine name so that all the cosmos will cry,

---

13. Terence L. Donaldson, 'The Vindicated Son: A Narrative Approach to Matthean Christology', in *Contours of Christology in the New Testament*, ed. Richard N. Longenecker (Grand Rapids: Eerdmans, 2005), 100-121.

'Jesus Christ is Lord!' to the glory of God the Father. The clear structure of descent and ascent, humiliation and exaltation, can be described using the mathematical analogy of a parabola, a line descending from infinity to a nadir or turning point and ascending again to infinity.

The hymn in Colossians 1:15-20 has the same cosmological background and the same elements of the narrative, though not in chronological order. There is the pre-existence, though this time as the 'image' (*eikōn*) of the invisible God and as the pre-eminent one (*prōtotokos*) of all creation by whom the powers of heaven and earth were created. There is his human life leading to the cross; resurrection is specified rather than exaltation, but the purpose is to make him pre-eminent. He is the head of the Church, and particularly developed is his role in the creation, both visible and invisible. The hymn in 1 Timothy 3:16 is more obviously a poem, since the narrative order gives way to the figure of speech of *chiasmus* in which events in the transcendent realm alternate with events in this world. Interestingly, these hymnic passages are not confined to the Pauline letters. Bultmann suggested that another could be detected, quoted in various parts in 1 Peter 1:20 and 3:18 and 3:22. Two much more obvious 'hymn' passages occur in the opening verses of the letter to the Hebrews and in the Prologue to John's Gospel.

Whether Paul composed the Christological hymns in his epistles or is quoting them, it is clear that they represent his doctrine of Christ. Paul's Theology has been the subject of numerous studies, and there has been considerable debate about the 'centre' of his Theology. Lutheran scholars have tended to see 'justification by faith' as the centre, but for others that is more of a vital implication. It is particularly important to Paul as the apostle to the gentiles, insisting that it is faith, not the good works of the Law of Moses, by which we are justified. The 'new perspective' on Paul, associated with E.P. Sanders, James Dunn, and N.T. Wright, has emphasized a 'salvation history' approach placing the new covenant in the context of Israel. But the Gospel itself, which Paul shared with the other apostles, was, as we have noted, 'the gospel of God', which was 'the gospel of his Son'. Paul was not primarily devoted to a doctrine or principle (even 'justification by faith'), but his devotion was centred on a person, Jesus Christ.

Gordon Fee devoted one work specifically to Paul's doctrine of Christ.[14] It is inseparable from his doctrine of salvation, which moves from the love of the Father to the death and resurrection of the Son to the work of the Spirit. The pre-existence and Incarnation of the Son are essential for this goal to be achieved, and therefore (Fee concludes), Paul does not argue *to* the deity of Christ. He argues *from* it. Fee considers nine major texts in Paul on pre-existence and Incarnation. It may be possible to argue for a non-incarnational view of one or two, but one cannot overthrow the cumulative effect of all these taken together.

Fee also examines the true *humanity* of the Saviour in Paul's thought, beginning with his allusions to Christ as the second or 'last' Adam. The fact that the risen Christ continues to have a body now fitted for the life of the Spirit means that he is the progenitor of the *new* humanity. Paul's Christology cannot be divorced from his soteriology, but his soteriology is totally dependent not only on the full *deity* of Christ but also on his full *humanity* as the Second Adam in whom the image of God is restored. It is only as we are *in Christ*, crucified and risen, that we can be included in the new *humanity* in the new creation of the age to come. Soteriology, the doctrine of salvation, and Christology, the doctrine of the Person of Christ (who he is), cannot be divorced.

'One-in-Two' in the Synoptic Gospels

Turning back again to the three Synoptic Gospels, we are interested now, not in what they tell us of Jesus' own preaching of the Gospel of the kingdom, but in how the writers themselves tell the story. Writing after Paul, the evangelists share the same faith in the risen Lord, who is the eternal Son of God. But as is appropriate for those writing the life of Jesus, his *deity* is hidden as it was indeed during his ministry and death. Some modern writers have questioned whether the evangelists

---

14. Gordon D. Fee, *Pauline Christology* (Peabody, MA: Hendrickson, 2007).

believe in the Incarnation, since the word does not appear. But neither do the evangelists read into the passion narrative the later Atonement doctrine of Paul or the letter to the Hebrews. This simply confirms their concern to reflect what was actually said and thought during the ministry of Jesus.

Martin Kähler famously remarked that the four Gospels were 'passion narratives with extended introductions'. That may be an exaggeration, but it brings out the point that these four books are simply extended forms of the same Gospel of crucifixion and resurrection preached by the apostles. That is why they are called 'Gospels'!

What is evident is the basic one-in-two shape of the narrative. Focusing particularly on the three Synoptic Gospels, we can see the diversity in their approach. Mark highlights the question, 'Who is this?' given Jesus' genuine and real humanity. In Matthew, the mandate at Jesus' baptism to be the 'Son of God' confronts him with alternative interpretations of what that means, a tension resolved in choosing the way of the cross. In Luke, the identity of Jesus is a continuing motif, but he is seen in an exclusive and reciprocal relationship with the one he calls 'Abba'. All three Synoptic Gospels tell what is recognizably the same story, with a consistent focus on Jesus' humanity while the deity is hidden. The language of Incarnation is absent; the concept of pre-existence easily missed. The ambiguity is not resolved during Jesus' life and ministry. But the fundamental narrative structure is that of cross and resurrection.

'One-in-Two' in Hebrews and John

The letter to the Hebrews begins with another of the Christological 'hymns' with the same characteristics of those we have noted in Paul's writing. It has the same structure and cosmic background and the same one-in-two structure. Like them, it begins with a relative pronoun (whom) and speaks of the role of the Son in creation. Where they refer to the 'form' or the 'image' of God, this hymn speaks of Christ as the 'radiance' or 'reflection' (*apaugasma*) of his glory and the very 'stamp' (character, image, mark, figure, or imprint) of his being (*hypostaseōs*). The reference to the incarnate life is very brief ('When he had made purification for sins') and goes on immediately to his exaltation ('he sat down at the right hand of the Majesty on high') (Heb. 1:3).

But Hebrews 2 complements this with one of the strongest extended passages in the New Testament on the significance of his true humanity. He participated fully in what was common to those he came to redeem, namely 'flesh and blood' (v. 14). Only in this way (i.e., Incarnation) could he save his brothers and sisters from death and become the high priest who made expiation or propitiation for their sins. The rest of the epistle develops the theme of sacrifice and priesthood more fully than any other book of the New Testament, but it is inseparable from the full deity and the full humanity of Christ. What Christ did is inseparable from who he is. First Peter, as we have seen, contains another of the Christological hymns, albeit in interpolated phrases (1 Pet. 1:20 and in 3:18-22).

But finally, the writings known as the Johannine literature—that is, the Fourth Gospel, the Johannine epistles, and the Revelation of John—share in the one-in-two Gospel. The Prologue to the Gospel of John has been classified as the sixth Christological hymn, and it clearly bears the characteristic marks. It begins with the One who is in eternity with God, and it appears that the writer is consciously echoing the language of Genesis 1:1: 'In the beginning'. Instead of 'form' or 'image', we have the 'Word' of God, a word that scholars now interpret not against a Greek background but against the figure of the 'Word' or the 'Wisdom' of God in the Old Testament. There is a distinction between the 'Word' and 'God', and yet the Word 'is' God and was the Creator of all things.

Pre-existence is followed by express and explicit Incarnation: 'And the Word became flesh' (John 1:14).[15] It might appear that the hymn ends there abruptly without completing the rest of the one-in-two narrative. But a moment's thought reveals that the rest of the story is in fact completed by the rest of John's Gospel. What has happened in other words is that the narrative of the other hymns has been extended into a book. The incarnate life of Christ follows, leading to the cru-

---

15. The English word 'incarnation' comes from the Latin word for 'flesh', *caro*. It literally means 'enfleshment'.

cifixion. That in turn is subverted by the action of God, and resurrection follows. And although ascension is not narrated as such, but appears 'off-stage' as it were (like the baptism), it completes the parabolic movement of descent and ascent. This of course is in itself a Johannine motif—descent and ascent, below and above, coming from and going to the Father. The one-in-two parabolic structure of the hymns remains the one-in-two structure of the whole Gospel of John.

As befits a Gospel in which the parabolic shape is more evident than in any other, the assertions of *deity* are more evident and yet remain controversial during the ministry of Jesus. It only becomes a full outright confession after the resurrection. According to Richard Bauckham, the Gospel of John bears out his thesis that right from the beginning of the Church, a 'high' Christology and Jewish monotheism were not seen as contradictory. Jesus is included within the unique divine identity as understood by Jewish monotheism.[16] There are seven 'I am' sayings with predicates ('the good shepherd', etc.) and seven absolute 'I am' sayings, one of which, at John 8:58, is regarded as blasphemous by the Jewish leaders. They are to be seen, according to Bauckham, as references not only to Exodus 3:14 but also to Deuteronomy 32:39: 'I, even I, *am he*; there is no god besides me' (NRSV; italics added). They also have to be interpreted against the background of the 'I am he' sayings of Isaiah 40 to 55. These 'are among the most emphatically monotheistic assertions of the Hebrew Bible,' Bauckham concludes, 'and if Jesus in the Fourth Gospel repeats them, he is unambiguously identifying himself with the one and only God, YHWH, the God of Israel.'[17]

The First Epistle of John echoes many of the themes of the Gospel, including the Incarnate Word, and particularly accentuates the need to believe that he has come 'in the flesh' (4:2), a rejection of Docetism. In the Revelation of John, the exalted Christ identified himself as 'the first and the last' (Rev. 1:17), echoing the words of Yahweh in Isaiah 44:6 and 48:12, and as 'the living one': 'I died, and behold I am alive for evermore'

16. Bauckham, *Testimony of the Beloved Disciple*, 239ff.
17. Bauckham, 247.

(Rev. 1:18). The one-in-two pattern of death and resurrection is central to his identity. Later in the book, the worship of the slaughtered Lamb becomes central to the worship of heaven, dramatically symbolizing the one-in-two pattern of the One who was dead and is alive again, who was crucified and is exalted to be included within the glory and identity of God.

The Unity of the Witnesses

The analytical scholarly study of texts is indispensable. But any field of study, any science, needs more than analysis. If we only have analysis, we can end up in a failure to see the total picture. Only an overarching hypothesis can give unity to the whole field. What we have tried to see in this chapter is the underlying unity *in the text* of the witness of the writers of the New Testament in all their diversity to the Person of Jesus Christ. The grand overarching unity of the New Testament lies in the narrative they all share, the one-in-two narrative that began to be told as the resurrection and exaltation of the One who was crucified.

What we find in these apostolic texts is the identity of the One who came among as truly *human*, who was anointed by the Holy Spirit and suffered and died *for us*. He is the One who has been declared by his resurrection to share in the eternal *deity* of the One he called Father. New Testament Christology therefore is not merely the analysis of isolated texts declaring his deity. Rather, the Gospel story gives unity to the whole field of study and that unity lies in the One-in-two whose identity is distinct from the Father and the Spirit but can only be known within the story of the Three whose identity is One.

FOUR

Jesus: God and Man— the Early Fathers

The question we are addressing is, 'Who is Jesus?' As a prelude, we began by examining what historical study may tell us about him. But confronted with the evidence for the resurrection, we had to examine the philosophical presuppositions behind the historical-critical method. 'Naturalism', explaining everything within the causes and effects of the natural world, is acceptable as a *methodological* rule in historical and scientific research. But the evidence for the resurrection of Jesus calls it in question as a *metaphysical* presupposition. During 'this present evil age', this *saeculum*, the action of the Lord God may be *hidden*, but the claim that he has been active, revealing himself in the ambiguities of the long history of Israel, and that this self-revelation has culminated in the resurrection of Jesus of Nazareth, challenges us to respond in faith.

It is not just that the evidence for his resurrection leaves no credible 'natural' explanation. It is the life and teaching of this man, revealing 'Who' he is—his inexhaustible compassion, his fierce condemnation of hypocrisy, and his embodiment of the faithful covenant love of God. Confronted by him, a total conversion or repentance of the mind, a paradigm shift in our whole outlook on life, the world, and everything, brings us by the Spirit to confess that Jesus Christ is Lord. Here in this man is God Incarnate, risen from the dead. And so, crossing the threshold of faith in Jesus, and confessing him as Lord by the Spirit, brings us to acknowledge him as God the Lord in human flesh.

In making this move to faith in Jesus as the Christ, our guides are the apostles, that generation who witnessed his life, death, and resurrection. Their witness is embodied in the books of the New Testament. In the last chapter, we examined the earliest proclamation of the apostles, the Gospel, the one-in-two narrative of the One who was first crucified and then raised from the dead. We considered the fact that this oral Gospel was proclaimed immediately after Jesus' resurrection, first of all on the historic day of Pentecost. We looked at the earliest documentary evidence for this one-in-two Gospel in 1 Corinthians and Romans, and we saw how that Gospel was the presupposition of all the epistles and of the four Gospels. The New Testament arose out of the proclamation of that Gospel by the apostles. It was the proclamation of the One whose full and true humanity was evident in the cross and whose deity was revealed in his resurrection.

The Key Role of Patristic Teaching

The writing of the New Testament documents was not the end, however, but only a means to an end, namely, the proclamation of the crucified and risen Lord in the mission of the Church. The New Testament documents embodied the authoritative teaching of the apostles inspired by the Spirit, but that was only the beginning of the Church's mission of making Christ known. The New Testament did not mark the end of the proclamation of Christ, but only the beginning. The doctrine of Christ, the teaching we call 'Christology', has to be further drawn out and developed. Some have been suspicious of theology and have declared, 'The Bible alone is the religion of Protestants.' In the face of bad theology, that is understandable, but it is wrong. It was not the view of the Protestant Reformers, nor was it the view of the Wesleys two centuries later. The Bible is our authority, but it has to be properly interpreted and the truth of the Gospel explained and applied. We do not merely read the Bible in worship: we interpret and explain it as we preach. We therefore need good Church Theology.

Church doctrine therefore had a necessary role right from those who succeeded the apostles. The preachers and teachers of the Church had a twofold task: first, to safeguard the truth against distortion, and secondly, to explore and explain and interpret the truth and re-express it in new languages and cultures as these were evangelized. The meaning of the

Gospel of Christ, truly human and truly God, has to be explained and interpreted and *contextualized* in every generation and in every new culture to which it comes. Christology therefore does not end with the proclamation of the apostles. They remain the authority, but what they say has to be interpreted and contextualized and further clarified and developed.

The primary example of *contextualization* is to be seen within the pages of the New Testament itself.[1] In what is called 'the gentile mission', Paul and Barnabas and the other apostles *contextualized* the Gospel, first preached by Jews to Jews, in the Graeco-Roman culture. Under the inspiration of the Holy Spirit, they formulated new language and concepts in their preaching and writing. That contextualization was incorporated within the New Testament and invested with apostolic authority, but the task of contextualization did not end with the death of the apostles. Yet the apostolic teaching authoritatively laid down the lines of the trajectory.

Contextualizing the Gospel

Those who carried on the mission of the Church, the preachers, teachers, and bishops of the early centuries, known historically as the 'Church Fathers', were those who carried on this further contextualization. The teaching of the apostles, inspired by the Spirit and incorporated in the books of the New Testament, was authoritative for them. They were quite clear that they were adding nothing to it, no new doctrine. But it is not enough simply to quote New Testament Scripture. No document, not even inspired Scripture, can give an *exhaustive* statement of the truth. All reality is necessarily greater than our understanding of it so that no one can ever tell the 'whole truth' about anything. There is always more to be said. And if that is true of earthly things, how much more of heavenly! Even without crossing cultural barriers, the Gospel always challenges us to think more deeply about its truth and its implications.

---

1. See Dean Flemming, *Contextualization in the New Testament: Patterns for Theology and Mission* (Downers Grove, IL: IVP, 2005).

The development of what we know as Church Theology has a twofold purpose. First, it has to defend the 'true teaching' (*orthē doxa*) of the Church against 'other teaching' (*hetera doxa*) or 'heresy'. Secondly, it has to draw out the implications for our understanding of God and Christ and the world and ourselves. If Biblical Theology is the task of clarifying and expounding what is *explicit* in Scripture, Church Theology has the task of drawing out what is *implicit*—what is implied in Scripture for our doctrine and for our lives.

It is important to understand therefore that Church Theology is a continuous development over twenty centuries. We study it initially as Historical Theology, not as a metaphysical system, because the Word became flesh within time. And if we want to remain true to that mainline development over twenty centuries, we have to begin with the teachings of the Church Fathers and their doctrines of Christ and of God, drawn from the Bible and defended against the many ancient heresies. Protestants have tended to take that basic theology for granted and concentrate on other doctrines. But we can no longer do that. With old Christendom wasting away and young churches facing a variety of ancient religions and modern ideologies around the world, we have to ensure that we are firmly based on the patristic doctrines of God and of Christ, drawn by the Fathers from the Bible and defended against all comers.

That requires that we examine the history of the development of the doctrine of Christ. If we neglect this and think that we can simply look at the debates of the last twenty or thirty years, we will be wandering around in vain ignorance. We cannot jump from the New Testament right into the present day. We cannot possibly understand the present conversation if we have not followed the conversation from the beginning.

In this chapter therefore, we begin our examination of the classical Christology of the Church Fathers. How did they defend and expound the faith of the Church in the one Lord Jesus Christ, crucified in the weakness of his humanity and raised in the power of the Spirit to be acknowledged as Lord and God? Exactly how did they develop the Church's doctrine of Christ?

Questions and Options

It is helpful to think that the New Testament prompted this further development of the doctrine of Christ by, in effect, posing questions it did not explicitly answer. There are two questions in particular. The answer of the Gospel to the 'Who?' question—'Who is Jesus Christ?'—is the proclamation arising from the Gospel narrative of cross and resurrection that he is truly human and truly God. But how are we to think of that? All sorts of questions arise. Did he cease to think as God while he was in this life? Or did he never truly think and feel as a human being? Did he remain omnipotent or did he give up power when he 'emptied' himself? How are we to hold together the two statements that he was truly God and truly human? That is the *Christological* question.

There is another question that arises. How can we confess the deity of Christ and yet still confess monotheism, that God is One? Thinking about that question eventually led the Church to develop the doctrine of the Trinity, and in the end the two questions cannot be disentangled. We can think of the doctrine of Christ and the doctrine of God as two overlapping circles. Once Jesus Christ is confessed to be Lord and God, the two circles cannot be separated. The doctrine of God shapes our doctrine of Christ, but conversely, the doctrine of Christ now shapes our doctrine of God. We shall have to leave that aside at the moment, however. Our concern in this book is with the Christological question: Who is Jesus Christ?

Once we have embraced the Gospel and seen that his full humanity is implied in his crucifixion and his true deity revealed in his resurrection, we have to wrestle with what appears to be a paradox. Human logic rebels against paradoxes. We cannot accept what appear to be contradictions: they irritate us! We have a built-in desire to straighten them out and reconcile apparently contradictory statements. Right from the beginning of the Church therefore, there have been those who want to reject the Incarnation on the grounds that it is an 'illogical' doctrine. Claiming to belong to Christ, they nevertheless insist that the infinite God must be subject to their finite human logic, and so they reject the doctrine of the Incarnation on the grounds that it is 'incoherent' or 'meaningless'. But refusing the paradox of the Incarnation leaves only a limited number of other options.

To put the options as simply as possible: first, it is possible to reject or compromise the 'two' in the 'One-in-two', either the full deity or the full humanity. Secondly, it is possible to unite the 'two' so that they are One but no longer two. Jesus Christ is thought of as an intermediary being—a demi-god who is not quite God, or a superman who is not fully human. Thirdly, it is possible to hold the 'two' apart so that Christ is thought of as two persons in effect, a human being inhabited by a divine being. There are many variations, but these are the three logical options for those who want to reject the Incarnation but still claim to be Christians. These options were explored in the early Christian centuries as the Church wrestled with what became regarded as the heresies.

Bishops, Ebionites, and Docetists

The lives of the Christian leaders who followed immediately after the apostles are not well-documented. But the documents left by that next generation, known as the 'Apostolic Fathers', include the writings of three bishops, Ignatius of Antioch, Polycarp of Smyrna, and Clement of Rome. It is difficult to be precise about the range of beliefs in the earliest churches, scattered across the Graeco-Roman world and influenced by numerous cultures and traditions in that multi-cultural society. It would be facile to think that there was a clearly enunciated doctrinal unity. All kinds of wild and strange ideas no doubt permeated the numerous house churches. Nor had the canon of the New Testament been finalized. Yet the main outline of the canon, including the letters of Paul and the four Gospels were becoming accepted across the different provinces by the middle of the second century.

In the midst of the complexity and confusion, however, we can identify two early trends that rejected the One-in-two and adopted the first of the three options we listed. The Ebionites were Jewish followers of Jesus who emerged from the earliest churches in Jerusalem and Judea. 'Ebionite' derives from the Hebrew word for the 'poor', and we may speculate that they may have originated in the group of Christian 'Judaizers' who opposed Paul. In strong adherence to the Law of Moses, they denied the One-in-two by denying the true deity. In the late third century, a similar view seems to have developed in the teaching of Paul of Samosata, elected bishop of Antioch in AD 260. He appears to have held the view that Jesus was only a human being but anointed by the Holy Spirit and so 'adopted' Son of God at his baptism. Adoptionism was close to Ebionism in calling Jesus divine in a loose sense. But Jesus had not pre-existed his birth at Bethlehem and was certainly not to be identified with the one God.

The other trend that took the first option in rejecting the One-in-two was that of Docetism. But the Docetists held firmly to the deity of Christ while rejecting his true and full humanity. His body only 'seemed' (*dokein*) to be real. Whereas Ebionism was originally from a Jewish context, Docetism flourished in Hellenistic culture. At least from Plato onward, Greek philosophy and culture had a strong tendency to metaphysical dualism, dividing all reality into the realms of the spiritual or intellectual, on the one hand, and the material, on the other. In popular religion, that took the form of numerous cults and sects that modern historians have usually grouped under the heading of 'Gnosticism'.

These sects were marked by a strong dualism between spirit and matter, soul and body. Some of them thought of the upper realm of the spirit as a hierarchy of 'aeons' or divinities from the highest down to the lowest composing what they called the 'fullness' (*plērōma*). They tended to think of matter as evil, the result of an accidental creation by one of the lower aeons or divinities, and human souls were spiritual realities trapped in material bodies. Some human beings, those who were more spiritual, had within them the 'divine spark', a truly spiritual or divine 'soul'. For these elite, salvation was therefore escape from the nasty, evil body and the realm of matter to the heavenly realm of divine spirit. Such a context produced a truly contextual Theology! Clearly, the divine Redeemer could not have had a material body, for matter is inherently evil. Hellenistic dualism of this kind therefore produced a Docetic Christology.

Ironically then, Ebionites and Docetists shared a common presupposition. H.M. Gwatkin analyzed the logic perceptively: 'If he suffered,' said the Ebionites, 'he was not divine.' 'If he was divine,' answered the Docetists, 'his sufferings were unreal.'[2]

Gwatkin put his finger on the common premise or assumption: that the bi-polarity of the one-in-two Christology of New Testament Christianity was impossible. Assuming that they already knew what was possible for God, both Ebionites and Docetists saw the suffering of Christ and the claimed deity of Christ as incompatible. Beginning from that presupposition, they rejected the paradox, the *apparent* contradiction of the Incarnation. The 'One-in-two' was impossible.

Ignatius and Melito

Against that background, we may see the so-called Apostolic Fathers. None of these early leaders of the Church developed Church doctrine creatively, but their firm hold on the 'one-in-two' Christology of the New Testament is clear. In the epistle that Ignatius, bishop of Antioch, wrote to the Ephesian church on his way to martyrdom in Rome very early in the second century, he warns of heretics who are like 'mad dogs', whose 'bite is hard to heal', and adds,

> There is one Physician, of flesh and Spirit, originate and unoriginate, God in man, true Life in death, son of Mary and Son of God, first passible then impassible, Jesus Christ our Lord.[3]

Ignatius boldly embraces the 'one-in-two', the 'both-and', as opposed to the 'either-or'.

Melito, bishop of Sardis in Asia Minor, later in the century positively revelled in the rhetoric of the great antithesis demanded by the 'both/and':

2. Henry M. Gwatkin, *Studies of Arianism*, 2nd ed. (Cambridge: Deighton, Bell, 1900), 6.

3. Ignatius, *The Epistle to the Ephesians, 7,* in *The Epistles of St. Ignatius, Bishop of Antioch*, trans. J.H. Srawley (London: SPCK, 1919), 43, https://www.google .com/books/edition/The_Epistles_of_St_Ignatius_Bishop_of_An/H0j5ENyBd NkC?hl=en&gbpv=1.

So he has come to us. So, although incorporeal, he has formed for himself a body like ours. He who appeared as a lamb remained the shepherd. He who was seen as a servant did not renounce his status as Son. He was carried by Mary and clothed with the Father. . . . Appearing as a child, he did not deny the eternity of his nature. He clothed himself with a body, yet did not limit the simplicity of his divine nature. . . . As man himself needing nourishment, yet as God ceaselessly nourishing the world. He clothed himself with the form of a servant, yet did not change the form of the Father. All this was in his own unchangeable nature. He stood before Pilate and sat by the Father: he hung on the cross and supported the universe.[4]

Melito's rhetorical flourishes force us to acknowledge that the great mystery of the Word-made-flesh is beyond our understanding and can only be expressed in striking paradoxes. In another fragment we have of his writings, Melito uses the Greek word *ousia*, which means 'being' but is sometimes translated as 'substance':

For in that one and the same was at the same time God and a perfect man he proved to us his two *ousias*: his deity through the signs in the three years after his baptism and his humanity in the thirty years before baptism.

Melito is starkly clear that Christ is by nature 'God and man' and insists against the Docetist extreme, that 'he was *made flesh* in the Virgin', but also against the Ebionite extreme, that we must speak of the cross as 'the murder *of God*'.[5]

In addition to the bishops, there were those called the 'Apologists', philosophers converted to the Christian faith. They fastened on to the word 'Word' (*Logos*) in John's Gospel but also widely used in Greek philosophy. The greatest of these was Justin, who led a house church in Rome and who was martyred.

4. Fragment 14, in Stuart G. Hall, ed., *Melito of Sardis: Pasha and Fragments* (Oxford: Clarendon, 1979).

5. *Peri Pascha*, 54, 489, 710-11, in Hall.

Irenaeus: Christ the Key

It is almost impossible to overestimate the influence of Irenaeus, the Greek-speaking missionary who went from Asia Minor to the Roman province of Gaul (today's France) and became the bishop in the city known today as Lyons. He was the last major figure who knew the generation of the Apostolic Fathers, the generation after the apostles. His major work, *Against Heresies*, was written late in the second century to counter the influence of the sects we have known as the 'Gnostics'. But after writing two books against them, it appears that he wrote a shorter work, lost until early in the twentieth century, the *Proof* [or *Demonstration*] *of the Apostolic Preaching*. That work showed how the teaching of the apostles, summed up in the three-point 'Rule of Faith', gave us the framework for the Christian interpretation of the Old Testament Scriptures. Irenaeus then went on to expound this more fully in the three further books of *Against Heresies*.[6] Christian Theology for Irenaeus is essentially the interpretation of Scripture.

John Behr draws attention to some technical terms from the Greek philosophy of Irenaeus's day. A *hypothesis* was an underlying (*hypo*) thesis or first principle from which everything is viewed.[7] It has to be postulated and accepted by faith or it would not be a first principle! There is no such thing then as a neutral starting point. Of course, if the *hypothesis* does not work, we have to adopt another. The various heretical sects approached Scripture with their own *hypothesis*, their cosmogony of a hierarchy of 'aeons' or divine beings in the *plērōma*, and they interpreted the Prologue to John to fit that. It refers, they say, to God, the *Logos* (Word), the *Arche* (Beginning), the *Zoe* (Life), and so on. But this is not the *hypothesis* of the prophets and apostles. Irenaeus writes that they are weaving 'ropes of sand'! They disregard the proper order and connection of Scripture. It is as if someone took a beautiful mosaic bearing

---

6. This is the order of writing proposed by John Behr in *Irenaeus of Lyons: Identifying Christianity* (Oxford: Oxford University Press, 2013).

7. See Behr, 112-15.

the image of a king and played around with the tiles in order to turn it into the picture of a fox or a dog![8]

Interpreting Scripture

What then is the proper *hypothesis* for interpreting the Johannine Prologue and all of Scripture? Irenaeus writes that it is 'Jesus who suffered for us and who dwelt among us', who is himself 'the Word of the Father who descended', and who is 'the same also that ascended'.[9] There in the Johannine language of descent and ascent is the one-in-two narrative of the Gospel. John Behr comments that the paradigm used by Irenaeus and widely within early Christianity is that given by the apostle Paul in 1 Corinthians 15:3-5:

> I delivered to you as of first importance what I also received, that Christ died for our sins in accordance with the scriptures, that he was buried, that he was raised on the third day in accordance with the scriptures, and that he appeared to Cephas, then to the twelve.

Behr comments: 'This Christocentric reading of Scripture, focused on the [Passion] of the Christ, enables seeing the Scriptures [i.e., the Old Testament] as a mosaic depicting Christ composed out of different tiles.'[10]

At the beginning of Book 3, Irenaeus takes up the same point, that the Gospel of Christ is the hermeneutical key for interpreting all of Scripture:

> For the Lord of all gave to His apostles the power of the Gospel, through whom also we have known the truth, that is, the doctrine of the Son of God. . . . We have learned from none others the plan [*oikonomia*, economy] of our salvation, than from those through whom the Gospel has come down to us, which they did at one time proclaim in public, and, at a later period, by the will

---

8. Irenaeus, *Against Heresies*, bk. 1, chap. 8. This is most accessible in vol. 1 of *Ante-Nicene Fathers*, ed. Alexander Roberts and James Donaldson (1885; repr., Peabody, MA: Hendrickson, 1994), 326ff.

9. Irenaeus, bk. 1, chap. 9, sec. 3, in vol. 1 of *Ante-Nicene Fathers*, 329.

10. Behr, *Irenaeus of Lyons*, 110.

of God, handed down to us in the Scriptures, to be the ground and pillar of our faith.[11]

The term *oikonomia* (Latin: *dispensatio*) is used here by Irenaeus to refer to the whole plan or arrangement of salvation. This economy of salvation 'is not known simply from reading the [Old Testament] Scriptures, but only from the preaching of the apostles—that is, as we shall see, the Gospel proclaimed "in accordance with the Scriptures", so providing a "concise word".'[12]

The Gospel, which was the very heart of the apostles' preaching and the presupposition of the apostles' writings, is now available in their writings as the key to interpreting them. For the post-apostolic Church therefore, the *hypothesis* brought *to* the interpretation of the Scriptures, namely, the Gospel of the One-in-two, must now itself be drawn *from* the new Christian Scriptures, that is, the writings of the apostles collected in what came to be called the 'New Testament'.

Further on in Book 4, Irenaeus complements his mosaic illustration with another:

> If anyone [then] reads the Scriptures [in this way], he will find in them [the Word concerning] Christ. . . . For Christ is the treasure which was hid in the field . . . [a] treasure hid[den] in the Scriptures . . . , [for] He was [indicated] by means of types and parables. . . . And for this reason, indeed, when at this present time the law is read to the Jews, it is like a fable; for they do not possess the explanation of all things pertaining to the advent of the Son of God, which took place in human nature; but when it is read by the Christians, it is treasure, hid indeed in a field, but brought to light by the cross of Christ.[13]

John Behr sums up: 'At the heart of Irenaeus's exposition stands the person of Christ, the beginning and end of the economy, and the starting point for his theology.'[14] For Irenae-

---

11. Irenaeus, *Against Heresies*, bk. 3, preface and chap. 1, in vol. 1 of *Ante-Nicene Fathers*, 414.

12. Behr, *Irenaeus of Lyons*, 126.

13. Irenaeus, *Against Heresies*, bk. 4, chap. 26, sec. 1, in vol. 1 of *Ante-Nicene Fathers*, 496.

14. Behr, *Irenaeus of Lyons*, 122.

us, the key to the interpretation of Scripture, his 'hermeneutic', is the one-in-two Gospel of Christ, crucified and risen, fully human and truly God.

The Rule of Faith and the Doctrine of Christ

The Gospel of Christ is at the heart of the grand narrative of Scripture and therefore, for Irenaeus, the whole grand narrative is the story of the Father, the Son, and the Holy Spirit. As we saw earlier in this chapter, two great questions arise from the declaration that 'Jesus Christ is Lord.' The first question is how the deity of Christ is to be related to his full and true humanity. How are these compatible? But the second question is how the deity of Christ is to be related to the unity of the one God, monotheism. How are these compatible?

For Irenaeus, the answer to the second question lay in the 'Rule of Faith'. For the narrative of Christ, crucified and risen, is set in the middle of a wider narrative. This is the story of the Father, the Son, and the Holy Spirit. The Father sent the Son, who died and rose again and who sent the Spirit from the Father. That is the wider narrative that Irenaeus called 'the Rule of Faith' and which was eventually expressed in the full doctrine of the Trinity. But before it was a formal doctrine, it took the form of this narrative.

Irenaeus lays it out with various wording, but we may take this one that comes near the beginning of the *Proof* [or *Demonstration*] *of the Apostolic Preaching*:

> And this is the rule of our faith . . . : God the Father, uncreated, beyond grasp, invisible, one God the maker of all; this is the first and foremost article of our faith. But the second article is the Word of God, the Son of God, Jesus Christ our Lord, who was shown forth by the prophets. . . . He also, in the end of times, for the recapitulation of all things, is become a man among men, visible and tangible, in order to abolish death and bring to light life, and bring about the communion of God and humanity. And the third article is the Holy Spirit, through whom the prophets prophesied and the patriarchs were taught about God and the just were led in the path of justice, and who in the end of times has been poured forth in a

new manner upon humanity over all the earth renewing humanity to God.[15]

This is not merely an abstract statement of doctrine, but the faith into which the believer was baptized, having confessed his or her faith in the words of the baptismal creed, bearing the same threefold shape. It was not merely a statement *that* these things were true, but a declaration of personal trust as the believer was baptized *into* the name of Father, Son, and Holy Spirit.

Given then that for Irenaeus Christ was the key for understanding the Scriptures, and given that this one-in-two narrative of the crucified and risen Christ was set in the context of the threefold 'Rule of Faith', how did Irenaeus understand and explain this key doctrine of Christ? What was his Christology? Who did he say Jesus Christ is?

Irenaeus's doctrine of Christ is in line with the 'both-and' or 'one-in-two' Christology we have noted in the New Testament and in Ignatius and Melito. But it is more fully developed in a comprehensive way, drawing out the implications. In Book 3 of *Against Heresies*, he set out his positive account:

> [God's] only-begotten Word, who is always present with the human race, united to and mingled with His own creation, according to the Father's pleasure, and who became flesh, is Himself Jesus Christ our Lord, who did also suffer for us, and rose again on our behalf, and who will come again in the glory of His Father, to raise up all flesh, and for the manifestation of salvation, and to apply the rule of just judgment to all who were made by Him.[16]

Note how the whole Christological 'parabola' is present here as in Philippians 2:5-11. No part of the story makes sense without seeing its place in the whole story. The essential unity of the whole movement is made clear in another sentence from the *Proof* [or *Demonstration*]:

---

15. Irenaeus, *Proof of the Apostolic Preaching*, sec. 6, in *St. Irenaeus: Proof of the Apostolic Preaching*, translated by Joseph P. Smith, Ancient Christian Writers 16 (Westminster, MD: Newman, 1952), 51; translation altered.

16. Irenaeus, *Against Heresies*, bk. 3, chap. 16, sec. 6, in vol. 1 of *Ante-Nicene Fathers*, 442.

So, if he was not born, neither did he die; and if he did not die, neither was he raised from the dead; and if he was not raised from the dead, he has not conquered death, nor is its reign abolished; and if death is not conquered, how are we to mount on high into life, being subject from the beginning to death?[17]

But Irenaeus deepens this one-in-two narrative of descent and ascent by employing the concept of *recapitulation*, drawn from Ephesians 1:10. There, Paul states God's intention to 'gather up all things in [Christ]' (NRSV). To 'recapitulate'—literally, 'head up again'—was, like *hypothesis*, another technical term in Hellenistic literary and rhetorical theory. Paul also used it in Romans 13:9 to refer to the law as 'summed up' in the command to love one's neighbour. Irenaeus is saying that the significance of the *humanity* of Christ (contrary to the Docetists) is that it is by taking *our* humanity as the new *head* of the race that he saved us.

The Incarnation and the Cross

We need to emphasize that Irenaeus is not replacing the cross with the Incarnation as the centre of the Christian faith. Quite the contrary! Rather he shows how only a grasp of the Incarnation allows us to plumb the depths of the cross. The two cannot be separated. In his doctrine of creation, he had emphasized (against Gnosticism) that the human race was created by God's two 'hands', the Son and the Spirit. But now God unites himself to his own 'handiwork' thus becoming liable to suffering. Victory over evil and the 're-forming' of the human race was impossible for us, but

the Son effected both these things, being the Word of God, descending from the Father, becoming incarnate, stooping low, even to death, and consummating the arranged plan of our salvation.[18]

Irenaeus follows this statement with a collection of Pauline texts, identifying himself with Paul's claim, 'We preach

---

17. Irenaeus, *Proof* [or *Demonstration*], sec. 39, in *St. Irenaeus*, 72.

18. Irenaeus, *Against Heresies*, bk. 3, chap. 18, sec. 2, in vol. 1 of *Ante-Nicene Fathers*, 446.

Christ crucified' (1 Cor. 1:23). He quotes Paul's summary of the Gospel in 1 Corinthians 15:3b-4: 'That Christ died for our sins in accordance with the scriptures, that he was buried, that he was raised on the third day in accordance with the scriptures.' Irenaeus comments:

> It is plain, then, that Paul knew no other Christ besides Him alone, who both suffered, and was buried, and rose again, who was also born, and whom he speaks of as man.[19]

This whole passage from Paul, Irenaeus is saying, makes clear that the purpose of the Incarnation was to die and rise from the dead, 'for since by man came death, by man came also the resurrection of the dead' (1 Cor. 15:21, KJV). Irenaeus goes on to quote Paul further on the significance of the death itself. It is through the blood of Christ that we are brought near; it is the death of Christ which delivers us from the curse since Christ became a curse for us.[20] In the *Proof* [or *Demonstration*], the significance of the Servant Song of Isaiah 53 is crucial.[21]

One-in-Two At-one-ment

But for Irenaeus, the key point we must understand is that the overall understanding of the Atonement bears the one-in-two shape of Christology. Perhaps the most comprehensive passage in Irenaeus on the doctrine of the Person of Christ is also his clearest exposition of the Atonement. For Irenaeus, Incarnation and Atonement cannot be separated:

> He united humanity to God. . . . Had he not as man overcome humanity's adversary, the enemy would not have been justly overcome. Again, had it not been God who bestowed salvation, we should not have had it as a secure possession. And if humanity had not been united to God, humanity could not have become a partaker of immortality. For the mediator between God and humanity had to bring both parties into friendship and concord

---

19. Irenaeus, bk. 3, chap. 18, sec. 3, in vol. 1 of *Ante-Nicene Fathers*, 446.

20. See Irenaeus, bk. 3, chap. 18, sec. 3, quoting Rom. 14:15; Eph. 2:13; Gal. 3:13 (Deut. 21:23); 1 Cor. 8:11, in vol. 1 of *Ante-Nicene Fathers*, 446.

21. Irenaeus, *Proof* [or *Demonstration*], secs. 68-70, in *St. Irenaeus*, 91-93.

through his kinship with both; and to present humanity to God, and make God known to humanity. In what way could we share in the adoption of the sons of God unless through the Son we had received fellowship with the Father, unless the Word made flesh had entered into communion with us.[22]

By 'Atonement' we are thinking here of the original meaning of the English word: at-one-ment, or reconciliation. What is implied here is that the shape of At-one-ment is the shape of New Testament and patristic Christology: it is two-in-one or one-in-two. Two became one in the Person of the Mediator.

Irenaeus goes on in the same passage to explore the significance of Christ's humanity a little further. He makes it clear that he thinks of humanity not as some abstraction or Platonic form but as actual, concrete human life with all the conditions of living within real time, with its decisions and opportunities and stages of development: 'Therefore he passed through each stage of life, restoring to each fellowship with God.' This sums up in one sentence what he had already artic-ulated more fully:

> He therefore passed through every age, becoming an infant for infants, thus sanctifying infants; a child for children, thus sanctifying those who are of this age . . . ; a youth for youths, becoming an example to youths, and thus sanctifying them for the Lord. So likewise He was an old man for old men, that he might be a perfect Master for all, not merely as respects the setting forth of the truth, but . . . sanctifying . . . the aged also. . . . Then, at last, He came on to death itself.[23]

Here he attributes reconciling, sanctifying significance to the whole human life of Christ so that his death is not seen as an atoning act in isolation but as the climax, culmination, and completion, indeed, the unique perfection of the reconciling,

---

22. Irenaeus, *Against Heresies*, bk. 3, chap. 18, sec. 7. See vol. 1 of *Ante-Nicene Fathers*, 448, for reference.

23. Irenaeus, bk. 2, chap. 22, sec. 4, in vol. 1 of *Ante-Nicene Fathers*, 391. Ire-naeus sees Jesus as 'old' in terms of the life expectancy of the time.

sanctifying significance of his whole life. It was his obedience throughout his life that, as in Philippians 2, was obedience 'unto death, even death on a cross' (v. 8). But his death on the cross was the necessary completion of his obedience. Without the cross, there would have been no At-one-ment and no salvation. It was his suffering on the cross that brought his human obedience to ultimate, final perfection and so reconciled us to God: 'It is finished' (John 19:30).

Christ and Adam

In exploring the significance of Christ's true humanity, Irenaeus draws on Paul's unique use of the Old Testament figure of Adam in two key passages (Rom. 5:12-32 and 1 Cor. 15:42-50). His use of the concept of *recapitulation* in comparing Christ to Adam helps him to link redemption back to creation and to emphasize (against the Gnostics) that it was the same God who created us who now saves us. But in the midst of the comparison of Christ with Adam there is a significant contrast: the Word did not take his human flesh from the dust of the ground, but from the flesh of Adam. He was born of Adam's sinful race. It was essential that the Word of God should take that very flesh that needed to be redeemed and sanctified: 'for He, too, "was made in the likeness of sinful flesh," to condemn sin, and to cast it, as now a condemned thing, away beyond the flesh.'[24] The sinlessness of Christ is thus of saving, sanctifying significance.

It is also of the highest significance for Irenaeus that it was *as* such a human being, descended from and of the flesh of Adam, that Christ won the victory in temptation where Adam had been defeated. The sanctification of our flesh began in the physical birth that was simultaneously birth from above, birth of the Spirit. It was because he assumed our Adamic humanity, our 'nature' (*physis*), and raised it immortal in his resurrection, that there is an ontological dimension to salvation, salvation from death. But the sanctification of our human nature was carried through in the free choices of this representative Human, particularly as he rejected the

---

24. Irenaeus, bk. 3, chap. 20, sec. 2, in vol. 1 of *Ante-Nicene Fathers*, 450.

blandishments of the tempter. 'He became human in order to undergo temptation.'[25] And as we have seen, it was this free obedience of the man Christ Jesus that took him all the way to the completion of his perfect obedience on the cross.[26]

The key point we want to note here is that Irenaeus stands in line with the New Testament and with bishops before him such as Ignatius and Melito in his Christology of the One-in-two. We have seen that this is not the static picture that is sometimes alleged in criticisms of the later Chalcedonian Symbol, but that Irenaeus sees it as *a double movement*. It takes two to agree to set aside disagreement. At-one-ment requires both movements, from God to humanity and from humanity to God. But the key point is that according to Irenaeus, *both movements take place in Jesus Christ.* It is not that he is only the representative of God toward us so that we human beings are each left to complete the reconciliation for ourselves. No: that picture sees his true deity, but it fails to see his true humanity and its saving significance. What we must also grasp is that he is *the representative human being who completes At-one-ment from our side as our representative.* He is our High Priest who calls us to believe in what he has already done for us.

He is not only truly God: he is also the true Human, embodying the whole human race in himself. And what is more, this At-one-ment is not something the Lord achieved merely by actions external to himself, but in a double movement *that is embodied in his own Person as the One-in-two.* He is both God and simultaneously the representative human being, achieving At-one-ment in what one early anonymous writer called 'the sweet exchange', later expressed by the Reformers as 'the wondrous exchange'. In fact, we can call it a *reciprocal substitution.* It is most economically expressed in a sentence from the final book of *Against Heresies*:

---

25. Irenaeus, bk. 3, chap. 19, sec. 3, in vol. 1 of *Ante-Nicene Fathers*, 449.
26. Irenaeus, bk. 5, chap. 16, sec. 3, in vol. 1 of *Ante-Nicene Fathers*, 544.

The Word of God, our Lord Jesus Christ, through his transcendent love, became what we are that he might bring us to be even what he himself is.[27]

---

27. Irenaeus, bk. 5, preface. See vol. 1 of *Ante-Nicene Fathers*, 526, for reference.

Jesus: God and Man— the Later Fathers

Continuing to pursue the question, 'Who is Jesus?' we come to the teaching of the later Fathers. The faith of the apostles and the New Testament Church was in Jesus, crucified and risen, fully human and truly God. We have seen how the early bishops and teachers of the Church in the second Christian century maintained and explored the truth of this New Testament Gospel. Irenaeus particularly brought out the coherence of the whole biblical story. But the Church still had battles to face to safeguard the truth of the Gospel and explore its full significance. We saw how the issues could be summarized into two key questions: First, how can we say that our Lord Jesus Christ is God and yet still confess, 'Hear, O Israel: The LORD our God, the LORD is one' (Deut. 6:4, NIV). Secondly, how do we think of our Lord Jesus Christ as truly God yet fully human?

The third century saw some progress in considering these two interlocking questions. Two theologians were particularly influential in responding to the question of how Christ could be God and yet God be one. Tertullian in the Roman province of Africa and Origen in Greek-speaking Alexandria both insisted on the full deity of Christ. The Greek philosophical concept of the Logos was used to explain the Prologue to John's Gospel, where it is written that the Word (*Logos*) was 'with God' and that the Word (*Logos*) 'was' God. The Logos came from God and so was divine in a way that the creatures were not. Origen particularly developed the idea that the Son was generated from the Father eternally and not just in time. In this way they both contributed to the development of the doctrine of the Triune God. But these two great thinkers did not make such a significant contribution to answering the other question, the one we are concerned with in this book: How are we to understand the confession that Jesus is both truly God and fully human?

Indeed, Origen tended to compromise on both questions. At times, he spoke of the Word or Logos as divine but not as fully divine as the Father. And at times, he spoke of the humanity of Jesus as so imbued with divinity that his body glowed with an ethereal light. This is the origin, by the way, of the artistic convention of the halo, but it tended to compromise on the full humanity of Jesus. It was in the next century, the fourth Christian century, that Christology proper, the doctrine of Christ as both God and human, was at the centre of a great prolonged battle. And the issues were not fully settled until the middle of the fifth century.

This was no longer a battle against the outright denial of the Lord's deity, the view that the Lord Jesus Christ was merely a man, as the Ebionites and Adoptionists had taught. Nor was it a battle against the view that he was divine but not fully human, as the Docetists had said. It was against more subtle distortions of the truth.

The Arian Controversy and the Nicene Faith

The so-called Arian controversy broke out in AD 318 when Alexander, the bishop of Alexandria, disciplined Arius, one of his presbyters, for his doctrine of Christ. In response, Arius wrote a letter to Alexander that made it quite clear that his basic starting point was monotheism. 'We know,' he wrote, 'that there is one God, alone unbegotten, alone eternal, alone unoriginated.'[1] In the light of that, how are we to think of Christ? Who is he? Arius supplied this answer:

Before eternal ages, he [God] begot his unique Son, through whom he made the ages and all things. He begot him not in appearance but in truth, constituting him by his own will, unalterable and unchangeable, a perfect

---

1. The full letter of Arius to Alexander may be found in a slightly different translation in *Christology of the Later Fathers*, ed. Edward R. Hardy, The Library of Christian Classics (Philadelphia: Westminster, 1954), 332-34.

creature of God, but not as one of the creatures, an off-spring but not as one of things begotten.

It is important to understand that Arius was not an original theologian. Indeed, this statement is quite muddled. But he was merely stating what many people in the Church believed, including some prominent bishops. They were influenced by the hierarchical picture of divinities in their culture and thought of the Word (*Logos*) as an intermediary between God and creation. He was 'a second god', but not God himself. A similar view is held today by the Watchtower Society (Jehovah's Witnesses).

As the controversy spread, the new emperor, Constantine, called a council of bishops to Nicaea, near his new eastern capital of Constantinople. The council declared against the bishops who defended Arius and edited one of the several existing baptismal creeds to make it a definitive statement of Christian belief, the original Creed of Nicaea:

We believe in one God, the Father Almighty, Maker of all things, visible and invisible;

And in one Lord Jesus Christ, the Son of God, begotten from the Father, only-begotten, that is, *from the being of the Father*, God from God, Light from Light, true God from true God, begotten, not made, *of one being with the Father*, through whom all things came into being, things in heaven and things on earth; who for us humans and for our salvation came down and became incarnate, becoming human, suffered and rose again on the third day, ascended to the heavens, and will come to judge the living and the dead;

And in the Holy Spirit.

The key word was the word 'being' (*ousia*). They declared their faith in the full deity of Christ by saying that he was 'from the being of the Father' and 'of one being [*homoousion*] with the Father'. By using Greek words and concepts, they were *contextualizing* the Christian faith in their Graeco-Roman culture.

The Council of Nicaea (325) did not end the debate however. The bishops who agreed with Arius recovered their position, and the sons of Constantine who succeeded him were more interested in political unity than in the truth. Numerous councils issued versions of the creed over the next sixty years, and it was not until the Council of Constantinople issued a revised form of the Nicene Creed in AD 381 that so-called Arianism was ruled out, at least within the mainline Church.

Rather than following the details of that history, however, it will be more profitable to consider the writings of the major theologian, Athanasius, whose thinking, preaching, and writing finally established Nicene Theology as the true interpretation of the New Testament. He answered the 'Who?' question to say that our Lord Jesus Christ was one Person who was truly God and fully human.

Athanasius: Why the Word Became Flesh

Athanasius succeeded Alexander as bishop of Alexandria and remained in office (despite being banished six times by various emperors!) until his death in AD 373. In a two-volume work, *Against the Nations* and *On the Incarnation*, he laid out his doctrine of Christ.[2] The claim that the eternal Word of God became flesh was foolishness to Greek culture, since life in the flesh was despised. Athanasius argued for its rationale, since the whole cosmos was infected with evil and decay and it was therefore fully rational for the Creator to rescue it. The full biblical narrative therefore has to be understood in the light of the Gospel of Christ, crucified and risen, and conversely, the Gospel of Christ, crucified and risen, has to be understood in the light of the whole biblical narrative.

Why then did the Word become flesh and die for our sins? That was because there was no other way for God to rescue his creation. Evil is not the consequence of our being in the material flesh, as Platonism and Gnosticism assumed. God made humans in his image, giving them the freedom to respond to him. But if they turned away from him, they would inevitably perish, falling back by natural corruption into the non-being from which they came. The word for 'corruption' was the same word

---

2. For the full text of these, see vol. 4 of *Nicene and Post-Nicene Fathers*, Second Series, ed. Philip Schaff and Henry Wace (1892; repr., Peabody, MA: Hendrickson, 1994), 4-67, or, for the latter, *Christology of the Later Fathers*, ed. Hardy, 55-110, or any more recent translation.

used by Paul in 1 Corinthians 15:53-54. This was the inevitable consequence of rejecting the Creator, who was the source of life and being. Humanity was falling away into decay, deterioration, disintegration, disease, dementia, and death.

The Divine Dilemma

Thus, when these human creatures rebelled against him, God was placed in a dilemma. On the one hand, he could not with consistency abrogate the law established in his creation, and our repentance could not undo the natural corruption that had set in. But on the other hand, it would be unfitting and unworthy of God should his project fail. Only the Word of God who had created humanity in the first place could undo the natural corruption of our race, and the way he did it was by assuming our mortal, dying humanity and restoring it to incorruption. That has two implications. First, it must be the immortal God himself who joins himself to corporate humanity. Secondly, it must really be our corrupted, dying humanity he takes.

And thus taking a body like ours, since all were liable to the corruption of death, and surrendering it in place of all, he offered it to the Father. And this he did in his loving kindness in order that, as all die in him, the law concerning corruption might be abolished.[3]

The action of salvation is thus not completed by the Incarnation, but by his death and resurrection. The whole movement is the action of the Word as the representative and substitute for us all. Athanasius then marshals his scriptural support (2 Cor. 5:14; Heb. 2:9-10).

But there is another dimension to this. It is not enough that through resurrection we should have renewed existence in our resurrection bodies. We had to be restored to the knowledge of God. Athanasius explains this in terms of the *imago dei*, the image of God. But for Athanasius, as for Paul, *the image of God is Christ*. His argument follows the same line as Paul's in the first two chapters of Romans. We have rejected

---

3. Athanasius, *On the Incarnation*, sec. 8. See vol. 4 of *Nicene and Post-Nicene Fathers*, Second Series, 40, for reference.

the knowledge of God we had and have been overcome by our own desires and the illusion and deceit of evil, and so have become irrational. But just as when a portrait is spoiled it takes the original subject to come and sit again for the artist, so the Word or Son of God has come to renew humanity, originally made in his likeness.

Again the implications are clear. The full deity of Christ was essential to this. Even that great archangel whom the Arians imagined was the Word of God, but was actually only the first creature who created the others, would not suffice. For he would not bring the face-to-face knowledge of *God himself*. On the other hand, our Lord Jesus Christ must be fully and truly human in order to come right down to our level. Athanasius sums up God's answer to the twofold dilemma:

> For in two ways our Saviour had compassion through the Incarnation. He both rid us of death, and also, although he is invisible and indiscernible, yet by his works he revealed and made himself known to be the Son of God and Word of the Father, Governor and King of the universe.[4]

Christ Our Sanctification

Athanasius adds two important reflections on this. First, while Christ was 'in' his human body, he was not contained in it in such a way that he was no longer the Word of the Father sustaining the universe by the word of his power. Secondly, the fact that he assumed our corruptible, dying human nature from his mother did not mean that he was defiled by it or was in any way sinful. Quite the contrary! He sanctified our human nature in his own body. 'Therefore,' Athanasius writes, 'neither when the virgin gave birth was he acted upon, nor when he was in the body was he polluted, but rather he sanctified the body.'[5] He quotes 1 Peter 2:22: 'He did no sin, neither was deceit found in his mouth.'[6]

---

4. Athanasius, sec. 16. See vol. 4 of *Nicene and Post-Nicene Fathers*, Second Series, 44-45, for reference.

5. Athanasius, sec. 17. See vol. 4 of *Nicene and Post-Nicene Fathers*, Second Series, 45, for reference.

6. Athanasius, sec. 17, quoting 1 Pet. 2:22. See vol. 4 of *Nicene and Post-Nicene Fathers*, Second Series, 45, for reference.

In his later work, *Against the Arians*, Athanasius further develops his thinking that the full and true humanity of Christ was essential for our sanctification. The doctrine of the Person of Christ and the doctrine of salvation cannot be separated. The Christian's sanctification is possible because Christ took our humanity and sanctified it in his own body. We are sanctified 'in Christ'.

Athanasius proceeds to consider Christ's death, 'the chief point of our faith'. Only the Saviour who created the universe in the first place could bring what was corrupt to incorruption, and he did this through his death and rising again. He did so by paying the debt on behalf of all to make them guiltless, reflecting the fact that it was because of the law that humankind was under obligation ('debt') to die. As our representative and substitute, he released all humankind from guilt. Two things were thus accomplished: the death of all was fulfilled in the Lord's body, and death and corruption were destroyed because of the Word who was in it. Athanasius quotes 1 Corinthians 15:53: 'This corruption must put on incorruption, and this mortal put on immortality.'[7] For Athanasius, Christology (the doctrine of Christ) and soteriology (the doctrine of salvation) are inseparable.

Near the end of *On the Incarnation*, Athanasius sums up his doctrine:

> For he became human that we might become divine; and he revealed himself through a body that we might receive a conception of the invisible Father; and he endured insults from men that we might inherit incorruption.[8]

The concept of divinization or deification here does not and cannot mean that we literally become part of, or are absorbed into, God. Bearing in mind passages such as John 10:34-35, and the common notion of 'divinization' in the ancient world, it has to be taken to mean that Christians are brought into such a relationship with God that they reflect his

---

7. Athanasius, sec. 21. See vol. 4 of *Nicene and Post-Nicene Fathers*, Second Series, 47, for reference.

8. Athanasius, sec. 54. See vol. 4 of *Nicene and Post-Nicene Fathers*, Second Series, 65, for reference.

holiness. This is thus a statement of the 'wondrous exchange' just like the statement of Irenaeus that he became what we are that we might become what he is.[9]

Although Athanasius died in AD 373, the Council of Constantinople eight years later reinstated an enlarged and edited version of the Creed of Nicaea that he had defended throughout his long ministry. In particular, it reaffirmed the key word *homoousion*, declaring that the Son was 'one in being' with or 'of the same being' (*homoousion*) as the Father. The new version, while it showed the influence of his younger contemporaries, the Cappadocian Fathers, in the doctrine of the Trinity, was fully in line with Athanasius' understanding of Christology, the doctrine of the Person of Christ.

Alexandrians and Antiochenes

If the Council of Constantinople of AD 381 and its revised version of the Nicene Creed finally established the Church's doctrine on the full deity of our Lord Jesus Christ, it did not settle all the debates about how this was to be held together with his true and full humanity. Debates continued over the next seventy years, and we can identify two broad schools of thought that were in tension even though they were both committed to the Nicene Creed and its clear affirmation of the deity of Christ.

First, there was the Alexandrian approach, which we have just examined in the thinking of Athanasius. This tended to focus on salvation from *death* and therefore on the fact that it was our dying, physically corruptible humanity which the Word or Son of God assumed in his Incarnation, took to death on the cross, and raised again immortal in his resurrection. In Athanasius, this was undergirded by a Hebraic view of humanity as 'flesh', a perishing corporate reality as in the exclamation in Isaiah 40: 'All flesh is grass' (v. 6). This was the *ontological* aspect of salvation as salvation of our *being*, salvation from eternal death. It was less influenced by the Platonist

9. Irenaeus, *Against Heresies*, bk. 5, preface, quoted above in Chapter 4, p. 85.

view of the individual soul as a distinct entity, which, according to Plato, was inherently immortal.

In contrast to that, one school of thought (among several) developed in the church at Antioch in Syria. Here the focus was more on the *ethical* aspect, salvation from *sin*. And whereas the Johannine Prologue was formative in the Alexandrian tradition, this way of thinking in Antioch can be seen to be influenced particularly by the Christological hymn of Philippians 2. There the key to salvation is the *obedience* of Christ, 'obedient unto death, even death on a cross' (v. 8). Teachers such as Flavian, Diodore of Tarsus, and Theodore of Mopsuestia therefore emphasized that in order to be truly obedient, Jesus as a human being had to have a free will and agency. Without that, there was no obedience and therefore no salvation. It was this perspective on salvation that led them to emphasize the true and full humanity of Jesus.

In the past that has sometimes been caricatured as a 'Word-man' Christology in opposition to the 'Word-flesh' Christology of Alexandria. But that is now seen as misleading. Both traditions emphasized both deity and humanity. It is particularly misleading to say that the Alexandrians emphasized the deity and the Antiochenes the humanity. They both emphasized both! But the Alexandrians emphasized a view of humanity as corporate whereas the Antiochenes wanted to safeguard the personal agency of Jesus as a human being. For the Alexandrians it was vital that the deity communicated immortality to the humanity in a close union. The Alexandrians thus stressed the unity of the 'One Person', whereas the Antiochenes stressed the distinction between the 'two' and coined the language of two 'natures'.

Apollinarius and Gregory Nazianzen

Against that background, we can see the debate that arose over the doctrine of Apollinarius, bishop of Laodicea.[10] He stood in the Alexandrian tradition and was a respected

10. In Greek, his name was 'Apollinaris', but to be consistent here with other names, we will use the Latin version.

member of the Nicene party when he proposed a view of the Person of Christ that accented the close union. Unlike Athanasius, Apollinarius assumed a Platonist view of the human being as consisting of the body, the animal soul that provides movement ('animation'), and the rational soul or mind. In order to safeguard the full unity of the Person of Christ, he therefore proposed that in our Lord Jesus Christ, the divine Logos (Word or Mind) took the place of the human mind. The human mind was too defiled by sinful thoughts and so was replaced by the divine mind. This idea certainly safeguarded the vitally important unity. (And it may well be the view of many unthinking Christians today.) But this was at the cost of the true humanity. The Apollinarian doctrine was rejected as a heresy at the Council of Constantinople.

It was Gregory of Nazianzus who provided the reasons for rejecting it. Gregory was one of the three great Cappadocian bishops (along with Basil of Caesarea and his brother Gregory of Nyssa) who had defended the Nicene faith along with Athanasius. As archbishop of Constantinople, he had presided briefly at the council but had resigned (in disgust at church politics!). From his retirement in Nazianzus, he wrote several letters that succinctly expressed the case against Apollinarius.

'And if I am to speak concisely,' he wrote, 'the Saviour is of a "what" and a "what", given that the visible and the invisible are not the same, nor the temporal and the atemporal, but he is not a "who" and a "who".'[11] Nazianzen links that explicitly to the recent Trinitarian settlement at Constantinople, where Father, Son, and Holy Spirit are each a 'who' but are one 'what'. He is making the distinction expressed in the language that later became standard, differentiating between 'Person' and 'nature'. He then comes explicitly to the Apollinarian heresy and rules it out, articulating a fundamental theme of all patristic Christology:

---

11. Gregory Nazianzen, Epistle 101:20, 21 (author's translation). Gregory's Epistle 101 may be found in vol. 7 of *Nicene and Post-Nicene Fathers*, Second Series, ed. Philip Schaff and Henry Wace (1894; repr., Peabody, MA: Hendrickson, 1994), 439-43. For quotation, see the third paragraph.

For the unassumed is the unhealed, but that which is
united to God is indeed saved. If only half Adam fell,
then that which is assumed and saved may also be half.
But if the whole, I must be wholly united to the Begotten
and saved as a whole.[12]

Nazianzen was not formulating new doctrine here. This
was the agreed doctrine of all the Church Fathers. We have
seen it already in the teaching of Irenaeus that the Son of God
did not take his humanity from the dust of the ground but
from Adam's sinful race in order to save us.[13] We saw it also in
the teaching of Athanasius that Christ healed our corrupted
humanity in his own body.[14]

The sinlessness of our Lord Jesus Christ is therefore not
a merely negative reality, the absence of sin in him. Nor is it
only a legal reality, because a sinless sacrifice was required
by the law. Both these things are true, but there is more to it.
The sinlessness of Jesus was a positive, redemptive reality: it
was the sanctification of *our* flesh, taken from his mother. It
was truly a healing of sin-sick human nature in his sanctifying birth, brought about by the Holy Spirit; in his perfect
life, victorious over all sin and temptation in the power of the
Spirit; and in his perfect and loving self-offering to the Father
through the Spirit on the cross. Thus the full and complete
human nature and human life of our Lord Jesus Christ is the
source and origin of our salvation and our sanctification. We
are saved and sanctified 'in Christ'.

If Apollinarius represents an extreme Alexandrian
view—so emphasizing the 'One', the unity of the Person of
Christ, that he lost hold of the 'two' by losing hold of the full
and true humanity—Nestorius represented an extreme Antiochene view that was also rejected by the Church.

---

12. Gregory Nazianzen, Epistle 101:32. See vol. 7 of *Nicene and Post-Nicene
Fathers*, Second Series, 439-43 (fifth paragraph), for reference.

13. See above, Chapter 4, pp. 83-85.

14. See above, Chapter 5, pp. 90-93.

Nestorius and the Distinct Humanity

Nestorius was an Antiochene theologian who was briefly archbishop of Constantinople from AD 428 until he was deposed by the Council of Ephesus in AD 431. He so emphasized the distinct humanity of Christ that he appeared to lose hold of the 'One' and to be referring to two Persons. But recent scholarship has concluded that Nestorius was not really a Nestorian! The whole debate seems to have been bedevilled by confusion and to be largely a dispute about language and terminology. The dispute between Nestorius and Cyril, the bishop of Alexandria, can therefore be seen as a debate about two different ways of expressing the Mystery of Christ.

Looking back now from the perspective of our orthodox use of language, formulated by Cyril and agreed on at the Council of Chalcedon (AD 451), it is easy for us to fail to understand the problem. We know that the orthodox doctrine is that Christ is 'One Person in two natures' and that there are three 'Persons' in the one divine 'nature'. But in the century before 451, the terminology was fluid so that each side thought that the other was heretical because they gave different meanings to these words!

Nestorius was a stickler for logical precision, and he followed the principle of Aristotelian logic that 'secondary being' (*ousia* or *physis*) existed nowhere except in specific 'primary beings' (*hypostases* or *prosōpa*). In other words, human nature (*physis*) only existed in specific human persons (*hypostases* or *prosōpa*). That led him to insist that just as the divine nature existed in a specific Person (*hypostasis* or *prosōpon*) in Christ, so the human nature of Christ must have its own specific 'Person' (*prosōpon* or *hypostasis*). He therefore insisted on confusingly saying that just as Jesus in the Gospels presented one 'face' (*prosōpon*) to us, so when we discerned what he did as a human being and what he did as God, we discern two 'faces' or 'persons' (*prosōpa*), the human face and the divine face. Otherwise, he maintained, we were denying the reality of Christ's humanity. The problem, in a nutshell, is that the Mystery of Christ does not fit into the pedantic strictures of this kind of logic!

As their new archbishop, Nestorius provoked opposition among the people of Constantinople over their custom of referring to Mary, the mother of Jesus, as the *Theotokos*, the 'God-bearer', that is, the one who bore God in her womb. Nestorius objected to this. Mary did not bear 'God' in her womb, he asserted, but the human being Jesus, who was one with God. By no means, however, did his people mean that Mary was the source of the divine nature. What they were saying was that even in the womb, Jesus was God the Son. But Nestorius wanted to safeguard that distinction between the two 'natures' of Christ and so he objected to transferring divine attributes to his human nature or human attributes to his divine nature. In other words, as an Antiochene, Nestorius emphasized the 'two', the distinction of the two natures.

Cyril of Alexandria and the One Subject

Cyril of Alexandria, by contrast, emphasized the 'One', the unity of deity and humanity in Christ. At the council of bishops called to Ephesus in AD 431, he secured the condemnation of Nestorius for heresy and the end of his rule as archbishop of Constantinople. Cyril followed the Alexandrian tradition in asserting that there was 'one nature [*physis*] of God the Lord Incarnate'. He was using 'nature' (*physis*) in a different way to mean one concrete example, not common or generic being. But the heart of his case was (as some modern scholars have explained it) that there was only one 'subject' in Christ, one Person who was the subject of all his thinking and speaking and acting. The problem with Nestorius's way of using language was that it seemed to imply two 'subjects', the Son of God, on the one hand, who was in close communion with the Son of David, on the other. But we are not to think in this way of merely a 'close communion' between two subjects. Rather we are to understand that there was a full union resulting from the action of the Son of God in *becoming* the Son of David without ceasing to be the Son of God. The question this raised was whether Jesus as a man had the freedom to choose to obey his heavenly Father and could therefore act as a genuinely free human being representing us to God.

In the years after the Council of Ephesus, there was something of a reaction, and having established his case that Christ acted as a single agent or subject and not two, Cyril was prepared to soften his language. He accepted that the word 'nature' (*physis*) could no longer be used to refer to a specific individual human being, but should refer only to that common, generic humanity that all humans shared. He therefore accepted the Antiochene language that there were 'two natures' in Christ while still insisting on one 'Person' (*hypostasis* or *prosōpon*).

One way of understanding the difference between the two positions is to think of the Antiochene doctrine as insisting on a full *symmetry* in the doctrine of the Person of Christ. To do equal justice to both the deity and the humanity, we should surely say, 'human and divine natures' *and* 'human and divine persons'. To say, 'One divine Person, but two natures' appears to be unbalanced. It appears to give more weight to the deity of Christ and to undervalue his true humanity. However, that symmetry reflects a very *static* picture. In contrast to that, the Christology of the New Testament is *dynamic*. It originates as a narrative, a story. So in John 1:14, the Word *becomes* flesh. In the great hymn of Philippians 2, the one who was equal to God *empties* himself and *takes* human form. We visualized that as a mathematical parabola, which *appears* to be symmetrical. But in fact the figure of the parabola represents a *movement*. Thinking diagrammatically, we visualize it as a movement from left to right, the movement of descent from eternity down to death on a cross, and the movement of ascent up from the grave to eternity. There is therefore an *asymmetry* in the midst of the *symmetry*. And that is what is reflected in the language of 'One Person, but two natures'. We worship one divine Person, already God by nature, who additionally assumed human nature.

The Chalcedonian Symbol

The Council of Chalcedon met in AD 451, twenty years after the Council of Ephesus, and negotiated something of a compromise. It came after Eutyches, a presbyter in Constantinople, had been condemned for proposing an extreme

Alexandrian view, that the deity and humanity of Christ were mingled in the one Person. But the first thing we must note about the Council of Chalcedon is that it refused to formulate a new creed. Instead it re-affirmed the Nicene Creed as revised at the Council of Constantinople seventy years earlier. It then added a further explanatory paragraph to deal with the debates between Alexandrians and Antiochenes during those seven decades. This is the paragraph known as the 'Chalcedonian Symbol' or 'Definition', and it has been subject to considerable criticism. It did not even please everyone at the time so that on left and right, splits occurred. The Alexandrian or Coptic Church reverted to Cyril's original insistence of 'one nature of God the Word Incarnate', while the Syrian Church and others in the East refused to abandon the language of Nestorius and so have been regarded as 'Nestorian' churches. Perhaps the fact that some were displeased on both sides indicates that the Council of Chalcedon came as close to balancing the two as was possible! Even within the central position of those who accepted Chalcedon, debates continued.

But to make sure that we understand that the council affirmed the same doctrine of Christ affirmed at Nicaea in AD 325 and at Constantinople in AD 381, we need to note again the second article of the Nicene Creed, which they reaffirmed:

> We believe . . . in one Lord Jesus Christ, the Son of God, begotten from the Father, only-begotten, that is, *from the being of the Father*, God from God, Light from Light, true God from true God, begotten, not made, of *one being with the Father*, through whom all things came into being, things in heaven and things on earth; who for us humans and for our salvation came down and became incarnate, becoming human, suffered and rose again on the third day, ascended to the heavens, and will come to judge the living and the dead.

There is the same shape as in the hymn of Philippians 2—the unidirectional movement of descent and ascent, rooted in the original apostolic Gospel of cross and resurrection. What the bishops additionally devised at Chalcedon must therefore be seen as a further explanation, a footnote if you like:

Following therefore the holy Fathers, we confess one and the same our Lord Jesus Christ, and we all teach harmoniously [that he is] the same perfect in godhead, the same perfect in humanity, truly God and truly human, the same of a rational soul and body; of one being (*homoousion*) with the Father in deity and the same of one being (*homoousion*) with us in humanity, like us in all things except sin, begotten from the Father before ages according to his deity; in these last days the same [born] for us and for our salvation from Mary the *Theotokos* according to his humanity; one and the same Christ, Son, Lord, only-begotten; acknowledged in two natures (*en dyo physesin*) unconfused, unchanged, undivided, unseparated (*asygchytōs, atreptōs, adiairetōs, achōristōs*), the difference of the natures being uncompromised by the union (*henōsin*) but the distinctive nature of each being preserved and coinciding in one person (*prosōpon*) and *hypostasis*, not parted or divided into two persons (*prosōpa*), but one and the same Son and only-begotten God, Word, Lord Jesus Christ, as the prophets of old and the Lord Jesus Christ himself taught us about him, and the symbol (*symbolon*) of the Fathers handed down to us.[15]

True, this appears very static and to that extent perhaps somewhat misleading. The language of two 'natures' appears to dominate so that it is easy to miss the emphasis on the one 'Person'. The four great adverbs (as they are in Greek), *unconfusedly, unchangeably, indivisibly, inseparably,* seem to present a very balanced, symmetrical picture. The first two rule out the Alexandrian extreme of One but not two, whereas the third and fourth rule out the Antiochene extreme of two but hardly One. The static impression is not altogether wrong, since we are affirming that this is who our Lord Jesus Christ now *is* and will be eternally. But what is perhaps difficult for us to grasp is that he is who he now is because of what he has done. In

---

15. The original Greek text may be found in T. Herbert Bindley, *The Oecumenical Documents of the Faith* (1899), 4th ed. (London: Methuen, 1950), 191-93, and translations in Hardy, *Christology of the Later Fathers*, 372-74.

Christ, God's great Act was to unite himself irrevocably to his human creation.

The Will of Christ

One brief further point is necessary here. The real puzzle we have in our attempt to understand our Lord Jesus Christ is to think of his thinking and choosing. That is often put in terms of his will, imagining 'the will' as some kind of entity or faculty. Did he have one will (the *monothelite* option) or did he have two—one divine and one human (the *dyothelite* option)? If the latter, how did these relate to each other? This was the real problem for the Antiochenes: Did Jesus really choose freely as a human being to obey God, or was his human will determined and coerced by his divine will?

At first sight, it seems necessary to say that there was one will or to risk some kind of schizophrenia. But a little thought shows that that is not satisfactory, since it would mean that our Lord Jesus Christ is not fully human. Clearly this is a mystery beyond our competence. But artificial though it may sound, the Church agreed at the third Council of Constantinople (generally recognized as the Sixth Ecumenical Council) in AD 681 that we must say that the human will of Christ must be distinguished from his divine will. Maximus the Confessor (c. 580–662) had presented the arguments for this position. He distinguished, however, our 'natural' will, which characterized all human beings as created, and our 'deliberative' will, which resulted from human rebellion and sinfulness. As created, our 'natural' will would be characterized by love toward God, but human rebellion resulted in our fallen condition so that we were always pulled toward the option of disobeying God. In Christ, the human will was restored and energized by such love toward the Father that he freely and willingly obeyed at every point in his life.

By the end of the patristic era, the Church had not only safeguarded the New Testament teaching of the apostles in this Person, Jesus Christ, who was both God and human, but also explored the question of how we are to understand this. They had not come up with an all-encompassing theory that explained this Person. The Mystery of Christ remains beyond our ability to reduce the doctrine of Christ to a theory or to explain without remainder. But some specific distortions of the truth had been ruled out. Constantly changing human culture would mean that the truth had to be explored and re-examined again and again so that each generation could make it their own. 'Jesus Christ is the same yesterday and today and forever' (Heb. 13:8, NIV), but constantly changing human culture throwing up new questions and new forms of thinking has demanded constant prayerful thinking so that each generation may recognize 'Who' he is and adore Christ their contemporary.

SIX

Christ Alone: The Evangelical Faith of the Reformation

It may seem rather a big jump from the seventh century to the Reformation in the sixteenth century. But we have to say that in the Greek East and also in the Latin West, the doctrine of Christ saw no major developments. We need to note a few significant points, however, through the centuries when orthodoxy went largely unchallenged. All of these influence the way in which we answer the question, 'Who is Jesus Christ?'

Christ in the Augustinian, Medieval West

The great Augustine (354–430), bishop of Hippo in the Roman province of Africa, had immense influence over the Church in the Latin West, but he was not a particularly Christocentric theologian. He was orthodox, but the early Augustine was shaped by a Platonist piety that focused on 'God and the soul, the soul and God'. This lent itself to an individualistic, introspective spirituality that shapes much Western Christianity to this day. He was also creative in theological anthropology, the doctrine of humanity. He saw this in terms of the battle between 'grace' and sin, and conceived of 'grace' in a rather Platonist way as a force or influence coming from God. Using this concept, he battled against the heresy of Pelagianism and developed his own theory of original sin. The Church has always believed in the fall and universal human sinfulness, but Augustine invented the term 'original sin' and devised the theory that this condition, rather like a disease, was passed on through the lust involved in the conception of every human being. In his later life he developed his doctrines of Church and sacraments.

One area of Christology where he was influential was in his understanding of the virgin birth, or to be more strictly correct, the virginal conception. The whole Church had held from New Testament times to the belief that Jesus was born of Mary, who was still a virgin, by the creative action of the Holy Spirit. But Augustine proposed his own theory of how this secured the sinlessness of Christ. Since he theorized that original sin was passed on through lust, this neatly explained the sinlessness of Christ, since he was not conceived by action of a human father. While the doctrine of original sin is a necessary part of New Testament doctrine, Augustine's particular theory, connecting original sin and the virgin birth, is not explicitly supported by Scripture. It was connected to Augustine's generally negative view of human sexuality, and it was to lead in time to the much later doctrine in the Roman Catholic Church that Mary, too, was sinless through an 'immaculate conception'.

A century after Augustine, Boethius, a Roman senator in the age when Italy was ruled by the Arian Ostrogoths, was executed for his rejection of Arianism. In his work *On the Trinity*, he proposed a definition of 'person' as 'an individual substance of rational nature'. This rather Aristotelian definition became very influential in equating the concept of the 'person' with the concept of the 'individual'. In the eighth century, Alcuin of York (c. AD 735–804) was the leading theologian at the court of Charlemagne, the first king of the Franks to be crowned 'Holy Roman Emperor'. He defended orthodox Christology against the Spanish Adoptionists. In the eleventh century, Anselm (c. 1033–1109), archbishop of Canterbury, wrote his work, *Cur Deus Homo* (*Why God Became Human*). This attempted to show why the breakdown between God and humanity could only be healed by one who was both God and human.

In the twelfth century, the great preacher and mystic Bernard of Clairvaux (1090–1153) encouraged spiritual meditation on the true humanity of Christ. Christ's human love for us elicits our love for him and so for God. Bernard gloried in the 'exchange of attributes', particularly that in Christ, God has human feelings, hands, feet, and lips. Peter Lombard (c. 1096–1160) wrote the *Four Books of Sentences*, the theology textbook used in the medieval 'schools' for the next four centuries, shaping the kind of theology known as 'scholasticism'. He emphasized that the Mystery of Christ was beyond human explanation.

Thomas Aquinas (1225-74) is regarded as the greatest theologian of the period. His great work, *Summa Theologiae*, is an immense and sophisticated masterpiece, but, like Augustine, he is not a particularly Christocentric theologian. He differentiates 'nature' and 'grace' in an Augustinian way. The great scheme of his masterpiece is to begin with God and the creation he originates, to move to issues of law and sin, and then to move on to the dispensation of 'grace', eventually coming to Christ and the sacraments toward his conclusion. His doctrine of Christ is, however, a faithful reproduction of the Christology of the Fathers with some elaborate defence of the philosophical concepts they used.

Overall, the medieval Latin West was faithful to the Christological orthodoxy of the Fathers, but there was little creative theologizing in this doctrine. Instead, there was great elaboration of the Augustinian concept of grace, channeled to the faithful through the sacraments of the Church.

'Christ Alone' in the Doctrine of Martin Luther

The modern era begins with the Renaissance, that attempt to revive the great art and philosophy of the ancient classical world, and the Reformation, that half-successful attempt to reform 'the one holy, catholic, and apostolic Church'. Martin Luther (1483–1546) is therefore a pivotal figure in the history of the Church and of what we call 'Western civilization'. He formed what he called the 'Evangelical Church', which claimed to be in continuity with the ancient and the medieval Church in spite of the defects of the latter.

It was Luther's search for peace with God that led to his intellectual quest to understand what Paul meant by justification. Theology and Christian experience were therefore inseparable in his thinking and in his life. Justification by faith alone (*sola fide*) became for him 'the article [of faith] by which the Church stands or falls.' This was what led him to a Theology more Christocentric than that of Aquinas. 'Faith alone' had to be further explained by 'grace alone' (*sola gratia*) so that faith was not seen as a good work earning God's grace. That eventually made it necessary to assert 'Scripture alone' (*sola scriptura*) in order to reject the idea that the Roman church could devise doctrines not in Scripture. But the real heart of the faith of the Reformation was that salvation was 'by Christ alone' (*a solo Christo*).

'Christ alone' (*solus Christus*) was the equivalent of the *homoousion* of the Nicene Fathers, the belief that Christ alone was 'of one being with the Father'. The Fathers rejected a Hellenistic religiosity in which a hierarchy of divinities connected us to God, insisting that Christ alone was the Eternal Son, of one being (*homoousion*) with the Father. So also in the Reformation, Luther and the other Reformers were reacting against the late medieval religiosity, sweeping away the hierarchy of saints and priests coming between the believer and God. They insisted in the *solus Christus* that 'there is one God, and there is one mediator between God and [humanity], the man Christ Jesus' (1 Tim. 2:5).

As with the Fathers therefore, it was the pivotal role of Christ in the story of salvation that made Luther insist on the One-in-two, the one Christ in his true deity and true humanity. This is where the perspective of Luther and the other Reformers complements the Christology of the Fathers. Whereas the Fathers laid a strong foundation in the doctrine of the one *Person* of Christ as truly God and truly human, the Reformers more fully explored the *Work* of Christ, his Atonement centred on the cross. They also integrated the doctrine of Christ more fully with the personal faith of the Christian. This is seen in Luther's comment on the second article of the creed:

> I believe that Jesus Christ, true God, begotten of the Father from eternity, and also true man, born of the virgin Mary, is my Lord, who has redeemed me, a lost and condemned creature, delivered me and freed me from all sins, from death, and from the power of the devil, not with silver and gold but with his holy and precious blood and with his innocent sufferings and death, in order that I may be his, live under him in his kingdom, and serve him in everlasting righteousness, innocence, and bless-

edness, even as he is risen from the dead and lives and reigns to all eternity.[1]

The 'wondrous exchange' is expressed not only corporately but personally. So for Luther, Christ is the bridegroom, but it is not just the Church, but the believing soul, which is his bride:

> Christ is full of grace, life, and salvation. The soul is full of sins, death, and damnation. Now let faith come between them and sins, death, and damnation will be Christ's, while grace, life and salvation will be the soul's.
>
> . . .
>
> . . . By the wedding ring of faith he shares in the sins, death, and pains of hell which are his bride's. As a matter of fact, he makes them his own and acts as if they were his own and as if he himself had sinned; he suffered, died, and descended into hell that he might overcome them all. . . . Thus the believing soul by means of the pledge of its faith is free in Christ.[2]

Given this echoing of the 'wondrous exchange' we noted in the thought of Athanasius, it is only to be expected that Luther's Christology has a strongly Alexandrian flavour. If Christ through his death and resurrection takes our sin and death and in exchange gives us his righteousness and eternal life, then the accent will fall on the close union of deity and humanity within the one Person.

Following in the Alexandrian tradition, Luther has a strong emphasis on the 'exchange of attributes' between humanity and deity in Christ. This led particularly to Luther's argument that the human nature of Christ received the attribute of omnipresence or 'ubiquity' from his divine nature. This gave him a theological basis for arguing against his fellow Reformer Zwingli that Christ's risen body was not just in heaven with the Father but was actually present 'in, with, and under' the bread and wine at the Lord's Supper.

---

1. Timothy Lull, ed., *Martin Luther's Basic Theological Writings* (Minneapolis: Fortress, 1989), 480.

2. Lull, 603-4.

Luther's strong focus on the theology of the cross (*theologia crucis*), that is to say, soteriology, the *Work* of Christ, as the core concern of Christian Theology as a whole, was, as we have argued, a necessary complement to the patristic focus on Christology, the *Person* of Christ. It was part of his concern that Theology was not an abstract, academic pursuit, concerned with metaphysical speculations about God, but was embedded in the life of faith as dying with Christ. As one of his pungent sayings put it, 'A theologian is born by living, nay dying and being damned, not by thinking, reading, or speculating.' His soteriological thinking also had a strong focus on the justification of the *individual* by faith, largely lacking in the Fathers.

'Christ Alone' in the Reformed Doctrine of John Calvin

In Switzerland, the Reformation began, not with the discovery of justification by faith, but with a desire to reform the worship and life of the Church according to Scripture. The Swiss churches' more radical reform of liturgy and church government was indicated by calling themselves (in distinction from the 'Lutherans') the 'Reformed' churches. The Frenchman John Calvin (1509-64), who became the leading figure in the Reformed Church of the city state of Geneva and also the dominating theologian of the 'Reformed' tradition, was the first Reformer to attempt a comprehensive account of Christian Theology in his *Institutes of the Christian Religion*. It brings together in an organized, thematic way Calvin's understanding of the teaching of the Bible as he had expounded it in his series of commentaries on almost the whole of Scripture. The work is organized, however, according to the shape of the creed, and as with Aquinas, it is not so evident from this structure that Calvin is a clearly Christocentric theologian. It appears that, following the shape of the creed, the grand narrative of creation, fall, and redemption gives shape to the *Institutes* rather than the particular narrative of the Gospel of Christ.

Once he comes to consider Christology, however, it is evident that Calvin, like Luther, has recovered the soteriological perspective that was perhaps in danger of being somewhat obscured in the creed and Chalcedonian Symbol. Calvin begins Chapter 12 of the *Institutes* with Christ's role as Mediator: 'It deeply concerned us that he who was to be our Mediator should be very God and very man.' He goes on to articulate an Irenaean integration of Incarnation and Atonement that later Protestant Theology was too often to lose:

> Thus the Son of God behoved to become our Emmanuel, i.e. God with us, and in such a way that by mutual union his divinity and our nature might be combined. Otherwise neither was the proximity enough, nor the affinity strong enough to give us hope that God would dwell with us, so great was the repugnance between our pollution and the spotless purity of God.[3]

The 'wondrous exchange' of Irenaeus and Athanasius becomes the governing principle. The 'work to be performed by the Mediator' was to make 'sons of men' into 'sons of God' and 'heirs of hell' into 'heirs of a heavenly kingdom'. 'Who could do this unless the Son of God should also become the Son of Man, and so receive what is ours as to transfer to us what is his, making that which is his by nature to become ours by grace?'[4] That was why he had to assume 'a body of our body, flesh or our flesh, bone of our bones, that he might be one with us.' He who was to be our Redeemer had to be truly God and man:

> It was his to swallow up death: who but Life could do so? It was his to conquer sin: who could do so save Righteousness itself? . . . Therefore God, in his infinite mercy, having determined to redeem us, became himself our Redeemer in the person of his only-begotten Son.[5]

In contrast to Luther, who emphasized the union so strongly in an Alexandrian way, Calvin, like the Antiochene tradition, emphasized the integrity of the true humanity of Christ and its continuing distinction from his deity even after the union:

---

3. John Calvin, *Institutes of the Christian Religion* (1559), bk. 2, chap. 12, sec. 1, trans. Henry Beveridge (1845; repr., Grand Rapids: Eerdmans, 1989), 400-401.

4. Calvin, bk. 2, chap. 12, sec. 2, trans. Beveridge, 401.

5. Calvin, bk. 2, chap. 12, sec. 2, trans. Beveridge, 401-2.

When it is said that the Word was made flesh, we must not understand it as if he were either changed into flesh, or confusedly mingled with flesh. . . . He who was the Son of God became the Son of Man, not by confusion of substance, but by unity of person. For we maintain, that the divinity was so conjoined and united with the humanity, that the entire properties of each nature remain entire, and yet the two natures constitute only one Christ.[6]

This implies a more qualified acceptance of the exchange of attributes or properties. In line with that, Calvin denied therefore that the humanity of Christ actually became omnipresent or ubiquitous and so denied that the body and blood of Christ were *physically* contained in the bread and wine of Holy Communion. He asserted the *real* presence of the risen Lord at the Supper, but it was a *spiritual* presence, that is to say, a presence with his people in the power of the Holy Spirit. And while only those united to Christ according to the Spirit were members of his body, yet, contrary to some of his later followers, Calvin asserted that the full and true humanity of Christ implied that 'the salvation brought by Christ is common to the whole human race, inasmuch as Christ, the author of salvation, is descended from Adam.'[7]

Calvin was also more in line with patristic Christology, both Alexandrian and Antiochene, in insisting that while the Incarnation was real, it did not mean that the Word was *contained* within the flesh of Christ any more than the flesh and blood of the ascended Lord were *contained* within the bread and wine. While the Word was truly one with his own body in the Incarnation, and was truly active as a human being on earth, he did not abandon his role in 'upholding the universe by his word of power' (Heb. 1:3). The Lutherans dubbed this the *extra Calvinisticum*, but it was the doctrine of Athanasius.[8]

---

6. Calvin, bk. 2, chap. 14, sec. 1, trans. Beveridge, 415.

7. Calvin, bk. 2, chap. 13, sec. 3, trans. Beveridge, 412.

8. Calvin, bk. 2, chap. 13, sec. 4, trans. Beveridge, 414, and Athanasius, *On the Incarnation*, sec. 17 (see vol. 4 of *Nicene and Post-Nicene Fathers*, Second Series, 45, for reference).

Christ in the Thought of Owen and Edwards

The century after the death of Calvin in 1564 saw the emergence of what is sometimes called Protestant 'orthodoxy'. Common to both Lutheran and Reformed 'orthodoxy' was, ironically, a revival of Aristotelian logic and thus of the 'scholasticism' that Luther had rejected. In the Reformed tradition, this led to three developments. First, 'Federal' Theology (from *foedus*, Latin for 'covenant') proposed a 'covenant of works' made with Adam and the 'covenant of grace' foreshadowed by Moses but fully instituted in Christ. Secondly, Calvin's doctrine of predestination was developed in the speculative notion of several 'decrees' of God in eternity: the decree to create the world, the decree to save an elect portion of humanity and damn the rest, and the decree to fore-ordain the fall. There was great debate about the order in which God made these supposed decrees. Thirdly, since God willed to save only the elect, the conclusion was reached in the doctrine of 'Limited Atonement' that Christ did not die for all but only for the elect.

While this Reformed 'orthodoxy' was loyal to the Nicene Creed and the Chalcedonian Christology, these had in effect been relegated. They no longer gave shape to the whole of Christian Theology as in the Fathers. Rather, with these highly speculative innovations, Calvin's doctrine of predestination, elaborated in the novel doctrines of the covenants and the decrees, was what actually shaped the interpretation of Scripture and Christian Theology as a whole. This whole way of thinking was not shaped by the Gospel of the Incarnate Christ, truly God and fully human, but by these speculations about eternal decrees, which shaped everything.

Despite that, however, when it came to the doctrine of Christ, the theologians of Reformed 'orthodoxy' were, like Luther and Calvin, loyal to the doctrine of Nicaea and Chalcedon. The English Puritan John Owen (1616-83) was perhaps the greatest theologian in this tradition, and in line with Calvin, he strongly defended the true and real humanity of Christ.

Owen defended patristic doctrine against the Socinians, in particular the Englishman John Biddle (1615-62). Socinianism is historically important as the first significant appearance in modern times of the ancient Arian rejection of Christ's full deity. The Chalcedonian Christology of 'two natures' was logical nonsense, they said, since it was impossible for two natures with different properties to be ascribed to one individual and the Scriptures did not need to be interpreted in that way. The notion of the eternal generation of the Son from God was also incoherent, since it would imply the division of God's essence. Against this, Owen defended Nicaea and Chalcedon, making the important methodological point that human rationality is simply incompetent to judge what is possible or impossible for God. Revelation must have priority over reason, given that human language and logic cannot extrapolate from the finite realm of creation to the infinite and uncreated God. He defended Christ's pre-existence as God, the Second Person of the Trinity, and his role in creation.

It was particularly in connection with the office of Christ as prophet that Owen developed his insights into the intimate connection between Christology and the doctrine of the Spirit. The Socinians saw the prophetic office as Christ's proclaiming of the will of God, but for Owen, Christ can only reveal the Father if he is one with the Father. Humanity can have no true knowledge of God unless God is 'manifest in the flesh'. That leads us to the question, however, of how Christ as a human being can know and so reveal the infinite God, and Owen is quite clear that the finite mind of Christ cannot have infinite knowledge if it is truly human.

For Owen, the communication of divine knowledge does not come to the human nature simply by the Incarnation. Rather, it is the initiation of Christ into his office as Mediator when he received the fullness of the Spirit at his baptism that gave him the knowledge he needed for his task. In contrast to medieval scholasticism, which tended to say that Christ did not come to know anything through his human experiences that he did not already know as God, Reformed Theology rejected the idea that the finite was capable of the infinite (*capax infiniti*). Christ as man was therefore not omniscient, since the eternal Word was not *contained* within the flesh. There was therefore a real growth in knowledge in the human Jesus, but as the Spirit was the divine agent in creation, so he was also in the humanity of Jesus. This allows for the growth in 'wisdom and stature' indicated by Luke 2:52 (NIV).

Jonathan Edwards of New England (1703-58) stood in the same Puritan tradition as John Owen and embodies the link between Puritanism and the eighteenth-century Evangelical awakening. Edwards, too, emphasizes the full humanity of Christ in assuming our Adamic humanity. He wrote the following in a sermon on Luke 22:44: 'Christ, who is the Lord God omnipotent . . . did not take the human nature on him in its first, most perfect and vigorous state, but in that feeble and forlorn state which it is in since the fall.' And in the notes he kept for his own reference, he wrote these words: 'The [angels] saw him [Christ] in the human nature in its mean, defaced, broken, infirm, ruined state, in the form of sinful flesh.'[9]

Clearly this Reformed tradition of Owen and Edwards was echoing Gregory Nazianzen's insistence that 'the unassumed is the unhealed.' In no way did this compromise the sinlessness of Christ however. Indeed, it was precisely through the holy birth, life, and death of Christ that our human nature was sanctified.

Christ in the Thought of John Wesley

If Edwards represented the Calvinist element in the great Evangelical awakening of the eighteenth century, John Wesley (1703-91) and Charles Wesley (1707-88) represented the Arminian element and were also strongly influenced by German Pietism. Pietism arose in the Lutheran tradition as a rejection of dead scholasticism. It brought a new emphasis on regeneration, the 'new birth', but it carried the danger that Christians would become subjectively oriented around their own hearts rather than focused on Christ. Count Nicholas von Zinzendorf (1700-60) was the Pietist leader who welcomed the Moravians to his estate at Herrnhut in Saxony and gave them

---

9. Quoted in Stephen Holmes, *God of Grace and God of Glory: An Account of the Theology of Jonathan Edwards* (Edinburgh: T&T Clark, 2000), 137.

a strong focus on the 'blood' of Christ, which we see echoed in the preaching and hymnody of the Wesleys.

It is the strong conflation of the 'heart religion' of the Pietist Moravians and the *solus Christus* of the Reformation that comes out clearly in the well-known passage in John Wesley's journal in which he recounts the events of May 24, 1738:

> In the evening I went very unwillingly to a society in Aldersgate Street, where one was reading Luther's Preface to the Epistle to the Romans. About a quarter before nine, while he was describing the change which God works in the heart through faith in Christ, I felt my heart strangely warmed. I felt I did trust in Christ, Christ alone for salvation, and an assurance was given me that he had taken away *my* sins, even *mine*, and saved *me* from the law of sin and death.[10]

What we need to note here is that, having just listened to a reading from Luther, Wesley articulates here the *solus Christus* of the Reformation. The subjective experience of the 'warmed heart' was not the cause, but the consequence, of faith *in Christ*. The subjective feeling of assurance was a consequence of a response to the Christ who had died for him. This was assuredly not 'faith in faith', a subjectively oriented trust in his own feelings (although Wesley continued to wrestle with that temptation), but a sure trust and confidence in the objective reality of Christ crucified. It is no wonder then that he would frequently record of his preaching, 'I offered them Christ.'

Wesley has been accused of a slight Apollinarianism in his Christology, a failure to do justice to the full humanity of Christ, who truly thought as a human being. But while that may be a recurring tendency in orthodox Christians in reaction to the modern tendency to focus on the humanity of Christ, this is not a serious charge against Wesley's Christology. The charge arose from a misinterpretation of the evidence. Since the two brothers shared the same theological perspective, we may surely take Charles's Christology in his immense

---

10. John Wesley, *The Works of John Wesley*, vol. 18, *Journals and Diaries I (1735-1738)*, ed. William R. Ward and Richard P. Heitzenrater (Nashville: Abingdon, 1988), 249-50 (Wesley's own italics).

collection of hymns as a clear indication also of John's doctrine. Here the full deity, full humanity, and complete unity of Chalcedonian Christology are expressed with all the amazing versifying skill of English poetry of the Augustan age.

Christ in the Thought of William Burt Pope

The Reformation gave birth to the Evangelical tradition in its many forms—Lutheran, Reformed, Anglican, and Anabaptist. Some new notes came in the Evangelical Revival or awakening of the eighteenth century from which the Wesleyan tradition arose. The particular characteristics coming out of the Revival have been identified as conversionism, activism, Biblicism, and crucicentrism.[11] The last of these—the emphasis particularly on the cross and thus on soteriology (the doctrine of salvation)—tended to mean that the focus was on the Work of Christ rather than on his Person. Indeed, Christology seems to have been often taken for granted. The Wesleyan tradition seems to have shared that feature with the others.

Richard Watson (1781–1833), the first Methodist to write a Systematic Theology, had to defend the eternal generation of the Son from the Father against the noted Methodist scholar, Adam Clarke (c. 1760–1832). Clarke defended the deity of Christ but rejected the patristic doctrine of the eternal generation of the Son from the Father. For Clarke the biblical scholar, the title 'Son of God' only applied to Christ after the Incarnation. Watson argued from Scripture that the title 'Son of God' implied the doctrine of the eternal generation.

William Burt Pope (1822–1903) of Didsbury College, Manchester, following the footsteps of Richard Watson, defended the orthodox Christology of the Fathers and of the Reformation confessions. Before he wrote his three-volume Systematic Theology, *A Compendium of Christian Theology*, he had published *The Person of Christ*. He robustly defends the Chalcedonian Christology, distancing himself from the Lutheran view of the exchange of attributes and maintaining the distinction of the

---

11. David Bebbington, *Evangelicalism in Modern Britain: A History from the 1730s to the 1980s* (London: Routledge, 1989), 3.

two natures. He rejected the kenoticist view developing in contemporary Germany but strongly insisted on the centrality of Christology for the whole of Christian Theology.

For Pope, Christology is 'the basis at once and the super-structure . . . of the whole', and he deplores attempts stemming from 'jealousy for the atonement' to create a false rivalry between 'Bethlehem and Calvary'. The two must not be divorced.[12] The relation of Christology to 'the circle of Christian doctrine' is 'fundamental': any error in Christology leads to a perversion of the Christian faith and a 'perversion of its leading tenets'. It is connected to 'all the main principles of evangelical doctrine'.[13] Pope proceeds to demonstrate its vital importance for five 'watchwords' of Christian Theology—*revelation, mediation, sacraments, the union of the believer with Christ*, and *the Church.*

Given the pivotal significance of Christology, Pope carefully rejects all the ancient heresies. He follows the Antiochene and Reformed traditions in strongly asserting the full humanity of Christ and therefore his limited knowledge as a man, but he takes the stronger version of the sinlessness of Christ, writing, 'But in Him was no sin, nor the possibility of sin.'[14] In writing about the relation between the Incarnation and the Atonement, he keeps a certain tension. On the one hand, 'The Incarnation is not so much one of the stages or acts of the Redeemer's history as the necessary basis of all.' It is therefore possible to say, 'When the Son of God became man the human race was declared to be a saved race.' But on the other hand, 'The Incarnation was a means to an end.' Only with the atoning death was salvation accomplished.[15] On the question whether there would have been an Incarnation had there been no sin, Pope also sees truth on both sides of the

---

12. William Burt Pope, *The Person of Christ: Dogmatic, Scriptural, Historical* (London: Wesleyan Methodist Book Room, 1874), 38.

13. Pope, 38-39.

14. Pope, 21.

15. William Burt Pope, *A Compendium of Christian Theology*, 3 vols., 2nd ed. (London: Conference Office, 1879-80), 2:143.

debate. But it is for him a speculative question: we are in point of fact a sinful race.[16]

The doctrine of the Person of Christ is expounded in Volume 2 of Pope's *Compendium*, holding together the Person and work of the Mediator under the title 'The Mediatorial Ministry'. Under the heading 'The Divine Purpose', Pope is happy to use the language of 'covenant' and indeed of 'decree', but as with Calvin, there is one over-arching covenant of grace and one eternal decree of the redemption of the world that is progressively unfolded and is finally fulfilled in the Mediator. There is a slight problem with Pope's use of language (not peculiar to him) in that he tends to speak of the eternal 'personality' of the Son of God and of the divine-human 'Person' as 'the result of the union of the two natures'.[17] Since the advent of Psychology as a social science, and its use of the word 'personality' to refer to personality types, theologians have generally used instead the word 'personhood' as the more abstract term, since we are not referring to three 'personalities' in God in the more recent use of the term. In his other major work, *A Higher Catechism of Theology*, Pope formulates the mediatorial significance of the Person of Christ with Irenaean simplicity: 'As Divine He represents God to man; as human He represents mankind to God.'[18]

Christ in the Thought of H. Orton Wiley

H. Orton Wiley (1877–1961) was the pre-eminent theologian of the Wesleyan holiness movement in the early twentieth century. If A.M. Hills (1848–1935) represented the tradition as it was shaped by Finney, Wiley steered the holiness movement back toward a more Wesleyan position. Wiley was president of Pasadena College (now Point Loma Nazarene University), and when he finally produced his three-volume *Christian Theology* in the 1940s, it was a judicious work of thorough scholarship.

---

16. Pope, *Person of Christ*, 32-33.

17. Pope, *Compendium of Christian Theology*, 2:118.

18. William Burt Pope, *A Higher Catechism of Theology* (London: Woolmer, 1883), 155-56.

He regarded Christology as 'the very heart of Christianity'. One chapter included a 'Scriptural approach' that traced the events of the life of Christ in their theological significance and a historical section tracing the development of the doctrine in the Church with a brief account of the main Christological heresies.[19] Beginning with 'the miraculous conception and birth', Wiley quotes the Anglican Reformer Richard Hooker in saying that the conception was also the assumption of human nature by the divine Son. Scripture (Luke 1:35) implied 'that a change was to be wrought in the very constitution of humanity.'[20]

Since Jesus was not just another individualization of human nature, but the conjoining of divine and human natures, then: 'The instant human nature is conjoined with God in the person of Jesus it becomes a redeemed nature, and furnishes the principle of regeneration for fallen mankind.'[21] The implication, although Wiley does not spell this out, is the patristic doctrine that it was our unredeemed human nature which the Son of God assumed from his mother, but that it was regenerated and sanctified from conception. The humanity of Jesus was consequently 'spotless' and 'in some sense already redeemed', and yet the final perfecting of the Son for his redemptive sacrifice had yet to come. This perfecting came through his normal development as a human being. Wiley quotes Irenaeus: Christ 'sanctified every age'—infancy, childhood, youth, adulthood, and, at last, death itself. This was the unfolding of 'a pure and normal human nature apart from sin', for Jesus 'had none of the vitiating consequences of inbred sin.'[22] This does beg the question how Jesus could then be 'tempted on all points as we are', and Wiley returns to that in his second Christological chapter.

---

19. H. Orton Wiley, *Christian Theology*, 3 vols. (Kansas City: Beacon Hill Press, 1940-43), vol. 2, chap. 20.

20. Wiley, 2:148.

21. Wiley, 2:148.

22. Wiley, 2:149-52.

The second chapter is a systematic presentation of the doctrine.[23] A section on the deity of Christ recounts his pre-existence as the Second Person of the Trinity, the identification of Christ with the 'Jehovah' of the Old Testament, and Jesus' unique claims for himself. In the section entitled 'The Manhood of Christ', Wiley writes again of Christ's sinlessness. The succeeding chapter expounds the 'Estates and Offices of Christ', and two chapters follow on the Atonement, giving the biblical basis and historical development of the doctrine and a systematic account.

This chapter has given an extremely brief survey of development through the long centuries we call the 'middle ages' and a somewhat fuller account of the doctrine of Christ in the Reformers and their heirs in the multi-faceted Evangelical tradition. This concludes Part I, 'Jesus Christ in Scripture and Tradition'. In Part II, 'Jesus Christ Our Contemporary', we shall look in Chapters 7 and 8 at the challenges to the orthodoxy of Nicaea and Chalcedon in the modern era and then, in two final chapters, consider what we are to say today to the question, 'Who is Jesus Christ?' Informed by this background we have drawn in Biblical and Historical Theology, we will look at how we are to express our knowledge of Christ today. What shall we say to questions that arise, and how shall we express our knowledge in doctrinal or Systematic Theology?

23. Wiley, vol. 2, chap. 21.

PART II

Jesus Christ Our Contemporary

SEVEN

The 'Modern' Christ

The notion of 'modernity', that we live in the 'modern age', began with the Renaissance of the fifteenth century. Modernity may be thought to have reached its peak in the eighteenth-century Enlightenment. The Romantic Movement of the nineteenth century was partly a continuation and partly a reaction against that. The twentieth century saw a new pride in being 'modern' but ended with the proposal that we were entering 'postmodernity'. There was no clear agreement on what that meant, but it certainly meant a loss of confidence in the 'Enlightenment project', which was thought to have failed in many ways.

In this chapter, we shall examine the way in which this cultural context affected the Christian answer to the question, 'Who is Jesus Christ?' Could we still affirm with the New Testament, 'Jesus Christ is Lord'? Could we still say that he was one Person who was at the same time truly God and fully human? Could we express that in the language of Nicaea and Chalcedon, or did we need completely new language and concepts?

Specifically, we shall examine in this chapter the tradition that became known as 'Liberal' Theology. That is something of a misnomer, since it has little or nothing to do with liberty. To refer to this tradition as 'modernist' is really more accurate. Its great and laudable aim was to commend the Christian faith to the modern world and to the current generation. But of course the danger was that the Christian faith would be fundamentally changed to fit into modern ideologies.

Schleiermacher and 'God-Consciousness'

F.D.E. Schleiermacher (1768–1834) was a German pastor and professor who had been brought up among the Moravian Pietists at Herrnhut, the settlement that had been founded by Zinzendorf. Decades previously, John Wesley had found spiritual guidance there.

Schleiermacher accepted, following Kant's philosophy, that we could have no knowledge of God as such. Theology was not therefore 'the science of God' and should make no such claims. What we could know, however, was the piety or religious feeling within our own souls. This was not merely emotion, but what he called *Gefühl*, a German word that means 'feeling' in the sense of 'consciousness', 'awareness'. This was true religious piety, and it was an 'inner experience' present in every human being even before we gave expression to it or talked about it. True piety was to feel or be aware of the Infinite in the finite, the Eternal in the temporal. In a word, it was 'God-consciousness'.

Schleiermacher had a very worthy apologetic motive in all this, expressed in the title of his first major book, *Speeches on Religion to Its Cultured Despisers*. His approach resonated with the new cultural tide of Romanticism with its rejection of what was seen as the cold abstract reasoning of the Enlightenment. Instead, Romanticism gave priority to the historical and the particular and the place of sentiment and emotion and feeling and knowledge through sympathetic understanding. To speak to this, Schleiermacher drew on his Pietist roots, but in fact he turned Pietism on its head.

For the Pietists, as for Wesley and the Methodists, true religion or piety was the believing response to the truth of the Gospel of Christ, crucified and risen, a subjective response to the objective truth. But for Schleiermacher, it was our piety and 'religious' feeling that were the beginning of faith and theology. The Christian 'religion' was, in his view, the highest of the religions, but the implication was that all were valid.

The Role of Christ

What was specific to the Christian religion was its relation to Christ:

Christianity is a monotheistic faith, belonging to the teleological type of religion, and is essentially distinguished from other such faiths by the fact that in it everything is related to the redemption accomplished by Jesus of Nazareth.[1]

That appears to make Schleiermacher's theology Christ-centred, and in a sense it did. But what we need to note is how he understood 'redemption'. For Schleiermacher, redemption was not centred on Christ crucified and risen, but on Christ as the one who had supreme *God-consciousness*. That was what was meant by the 'deity' of Christ—his perfect God-consciousness. What mattered for Schleiermacher was not so much the Incarnation, cross and resurrection, Christ dying for our sins, but Christ's life of God-consciousness. He communicated that to his band of disciples thus founding the Church, and it was in the fellowship of the Church that we, too, could experience this feeling or awareness that *was* 'redemption'. As for sin, that was a failure to cultivate God-consciousness.

Given his understanding of redemption, the key question for Christology is, 'What must be true about Christ in order for him to have the redeeming effect on us that he has?' Schleiermacher is determined to remain within the boundaries set by Chalcedon, but without employing the 'inconvenient' concept of 'divine nature' or of 'duality of natures'. He also wants to hold together the work and the Person of Christ, but he begins in fact with the humanity of Christ. What Christ does to bring about our redemption, that is, our God-consciousness, is to make his own inner life as a human being visible to us.

The key question that must be posed about Schleiermacher's Christology then is this: Having begun with the humanity of Christ, does he actually reach a clear confession of his true and full deity? Does he confess that 'Jesus Christ is Lord'? It certainly seems as if Schleiermacher intended it to do so, but altogether it seems rather weak and sparse. He claimed a certain continuity with the Chalcedonian Symbol. He identified four

---

1. F.D.E. Schleiermacher, *The Christian Faith*, trans. H.R. Mackintosh and J.S. Stewart (Edinburgh: T&T Clark, 1928), 52.

'natural heresies', Docetic, Nazarean (that is, Ebionite), Manichaean, and Pelagian, all of which he rejected because they conflicted with his understanding of redemption.

Perhaps all of the defects come back to the fact that Schleiermacher's version of Christian Theology does not begin with the Gospel of the crucified and risen Saviour and, in fact, has no true understanding of this Gospel at all. Sadly, it has to be said that Schleiermacher had a different gospel or, at the very least, a gospel distorted by the apologetic task of contextualizing it, adapting it to the intellectual and cultural demands of his day and culture. Schleiermacher must be given all credit for his attempt to rescue the Christian faith in the context of the Enlightenment and its aftermath. His genius inaugurated a new era in Theology, and his sincerity is beyond question.

Christ according to Hegel

Whereas Schleiermacher met the challenge of the Enlightenment by embracing the tide of Romanticism and beginning from religious 'feeling' and intuition, G.W.F. Hegel (1770–1831) met the challenge by a bold assertion of a new form of rationalism or Idealism. But he seemed to make Theology the handmaid of Philosophy.

Hegel denied point-blank the claim of empiricism that sense perception was the only source of knowledge. His bold claim was that 'the Idea' behind human history was 'the Real'—not matter, but *Geist*—Spirit. It was in fact the Absolute, even the sole Reality, the inner being of the world process or history in which it—*Geist*, Mind or Spirit—was coming to self-awareness. Hegel is thus the originator of *panentheism* in the modern era. The world is created as the Hegelian god's opposite, but Hegel's god 'actualizes' himself in (*en*) the world, hence *panentheism*.

For Hegel, truth was expressed in philosophical 'concepts', and the Christian religion was the pictorial presentation of this philosophical truth. The doctrine of the Trinity is then the pictorial representation of the action of the Absolute in the world process. The significance of the Incarnation is that the unity of divine Mind and the human has been made explicit in history. The universal philosophical truth of divine-human unity has been actualized in one man, and this does seem to imply an orthodox doctrine of Christ as truly God and truly human and a clearer affirmation of the Incarnation than we find in Schleiermacher.

But while this seems to affirm the true deity and the true humanity of Christ, in fact Christ is only a pictorial image of the grand narrative of the Absolute actualizing itself in the process of world history. The Christ-centred Gospel of the apostles is in fact relegated to the status of the supreme illustration of Hegel's panentheism.

Ritschl and the Founder of Christianity

If Schleiermacher and Hegel are the two geniuses whose brilliance seemed to offer rescue to the Christian faith, faced as it was by the onslaught of the Enlightenment and its aftermath, it was Albrecht Ritschl (1822-89), a less creative thinker, who was the dominant theologian of 'Liberal' Theology in its heyday. He rejected any kind of 'mysticism' or direct experience of God and sought to base the Christian faith in ethics. Pietism had been an illegitimate infusion of Catholic mysticism into the Protestant church, but truly Protestant Theology began with the 'historical' Jesus and his proclamation of the kingdom of God.

Given the alienation between God and humanity, the Christian faith is about *reconciliation*, which rests upon God's *justification* by grace. Jesus was the founder of the Church, the spiritual and ethical community whose goal was to transform the whole of human society into the kingdom of God. *Science* was about matters of fact, but *religion* was about *value judgments*. The declaration 'Jesus Christ is Lord' was therefore not a metaphysical claim about his deity but was simply a value judgment. It was a way of saying that Jesus has the value of God for us, since he reveals the love of God toward us.

Christology was therefore not a matter of metaphysical truth claims about divine and human natures: Ritschl rejected the Chalcedonian language as a false attempt at scientific or cognitive statements. The religious value of Jesus was in his conduct, his convictions, and his ethics, and to speak of his 'pre-existence' was simply to say that God foresaw and intended his coming and his work. For Ritschl, Christ's "uniqueness" is primarily to be articulated in terms of his being *the founder of Christianity*, thus possessing temporal priority over those who followed him. In other words, he was superlative but not truly unique.

Harnack and the 'Hellenization of Christianity'

Liberalism's most prominent representative at the beginning of the twentieth century was Adolf von Harnack (1851–1930). His thesis was that the whole development of the dogmas of Trinity and Incarnation in the patristic era were 'the fruit of the Greek spirit on the ground of the gospel', resulting in 'the Hellenization of Christianity'. This had begun as early as Paul, and therefore to recover true Christianity, one had to go back to the teaching of Jesus himself. The 'historical Jesus' was therefore the starting point for Harnack the historian.

Like Schleiermacher and Ritschl, Harnack seems to exalt Christ with superlatives, but when it comes down to his actual Christology, Harnack bases that on his own summary of Jesus' teaching. This comes down to three heads, each of which contains the whole:

Firstly, the kingdom of God and its coming.

Secondly, God the Father and the infinite value of the human soul.

Thirdly, the higher righteousness and the commandment of love.[2]

Jesus is the Messiah and the Son of God, but that does not mean what the Church took it to mean. It simply means that he had a deeper knowledge of God than anyone before him or has had since. But he remains essentially the teacher or preacher of the Gospel: 'The Gospel, as Jesus proclaimed it, has to do with the Father only and not with the Son.'[3]

Harnack strives to describe Jesus in superlatives, but there is nothing about Jesus' Incarnation and so nothing about his deity. The closest he comes is in the statement 'that here the

---

2. Adolf von Harnack, *What Is Christianity?* (Williams and Norgate, 1904), 52.
3. Harnack, 147.

divine appeared in as pure a form as it can appear on earth.'[4] Despite all his appeal to the teaching of Jesus in the Gospels, and all the superlatives he applies to Jesus, Harnack remains in the end of the day not even an Arian, but a Unitarian.

Walter Rauschenbusch (1861–1918) brought the Ritschlian influence to America where he became the main theologian of the 'social gospel' movement. He was rightly concerned with the extreme gap between wealth and poverty, but he attacked laissez-faire capitalism as part of the kingdom of evil and proclaimed the task of the Church to be the transformation of human society into the kingdom of God. Without actually denying the Incarnation or the deity of Christ, he saw the significance of Jesus in his teaching of a democratized conception of God by portraying him not as a monarch but as 'Father'.

Bultmann: The Bearer of the Word

The proponents of the old Ritschlian Liberalism of the nineteenth century, portraying Jesus as the founder of a movement for social reform, received one blow when Schweitzer demonstrated how their portrayal of the supposedly 'historical' Jesus was simply a reflection of their own philosophy. Their identification of modern Western 'progress' with the kingdom of God suffered a further crisis with the appalling catastrophe of the First World War. At the end of that, Barth led the reaction along with Emil Brunner, Rudolf Bultmann, and others. But that group soon split. While Barth and Bultmann turned to the Theology of the Reformation, Bultmann developed an extreme scepticism about the historicity of the New Testament and was strongly influenced by the new school of existentialist philosophy.

As a New Testament scholar, Bultmann (1884–1976) developed 'form criticism', an attempt to trace how the stories in the Gospels had been shaped and altered to speak to the concerns of the early Christian communities during the stage of oral transmission. His historical scepticism also derived from his view that 'modernity' must reject the ancient mythological

---

4. Harnack, 149.

worldview of the first century. In the modern world of electricity and radios and modern medicine, we could no longer believe in heaven above, earth beneath, and the underworld below, peopled by angels and demons. The Gospel had to be 'demythologized'. As a Lutheran, he identified the Gospel as justification by faith, but he interpreted what that meant according to the twentieth-century philosophy of existentialism. Here he was influenced by his colleague, the philosopher Martin Heidegger (1889–1976).

Heidegger was concerned with what he called *Dasein*, 'Being-there', the precarious givenness each individual feels about his or her life. To deal with the anxiety brought by the awareness of certain death, individuals become lost in 'inauthentic' existence, losing themselves in their daily concerns. To escape from this to 'authentic' existence, we have to face up to our mortality, our anxiety, and guilt and 'decide' to embrace the future.

For Bultmann, this was what Jesus did. He therefore was the Bearer of the Word of God. The *kerygma*, the message of the cross, was not objective information that God had literally raised the crucified Jesus from the dead. It was rather the proclamation that God has accepted us in our finitude and our guilt. This brings us the new 'self-understanding' that releases us to accept ourselves and make the crucial *decision*, not clinging to the dead old past with its false security, but striking out in faith to live *authentically*. Jesus did not literally rise from the dead in a new body, but the *kerygma*, the Easter proclamation, is an encounter with him, present in the word of the Gospel through which we are 'justified by faith'.

This is ingenious, but again we have to conclude that this is a different gospel. It is anthropocentric rather than Christocentric. It has no clear message of what God accomplished in Christ; it is individualistic, carrying no implications for the created world; and it has little claim to stand on the Christology of the apostles and the Great Tradition of the Church. Jesus may be the 'Bearer of the Word', but it is not entirely clear whether he is the Word Incarnate.

Tillich: New Being

Paul Tillich (1885–1965) also shared the apologetic motive of the Liberal tradition. He proposed the method of *correlation*: the world (specifically philosophy) sets the questions to which Christian Theology gives its answers. Once again existentialism set the questions about the nature of being, specifically the question of my individual death. Tillich's philosophical formulation distinguishes between *existence*, our actual existence in the world, and *essence*, our true being. Since God was true Being, true eternal essence, he should not be said to 'exist' in this world, but to be the 'Ground of Being'. Our creation in the world *was* our fall: to exist as creatures in the world was to exist as aliens to our true being or *essence* in God.

Given all that, the Christian message of salvation is that of the 'New Creation', that our 'New Being' is in Jesus, who has appeared as 'the Christ'. This does not mean that the Incarnation was an event as decreed by Chalcedon with two 'natures' in one 'Person'. Rather, the Incarnation is a *symbol*. Whereas 'signs' are arbitrary, for Tillich 'symbols' partake of the reality they represent. And yet we must not allow them to become confused with the reality they represent or they will become idols. The crucifixion was a real event that has become a *symbol* for Jesus' life of self-denial, but the resurrection is a symbol of the new life in Christ. By our self-denial, we share in this 'New Being'.

Once again we have a Liberal theologian of genius and great creativity who, in attempting to contextualize the Gospel of Christ in the 'modern' world, has ended up with another gospel.

Cobb: Creative Transformation

John Cobb (b. 1925) attempted to formulate his doctrine of Christ within the approach of 'process' theology. 'Process' thought has its origins in the philosophy of Alfred North Whitehead (1861–1947). He proposed that, following Einstein's scientific revolution, we can no longer think of reality in a Newtonian way, as discreet objects interacting mechanically, but must think of reality using 'field' theory. Reality should not be conceived of as objects, static 'substances' that exist through time, but as a series of 'actual occasions'. Each 'actual occasion' is dipolar with a 'mental pole' striving toward some value or goal and a 'physical pole'. Each 'occasion' perishes but is 'prehended' (grasped) by its successor. God, too, is dipolar. In his 'primordial' nature or 'mental pole', he envisages all possibilities for the future and seeks to 'lure' actual occasions to what is good. Yet in his 'consequent' nature, the temporal or physical pole, God 'prehends' the universe and becomes the location for all perishing 'actual occasions'.

John Cobb makes a sterling attempt to recast the Christian doctrine of Christ to fit this metaphysical system. Cobb proposed that the Logos, who became incarnate in Jesus according to classical Christian Theology, was God's primordial nature, that nature of God which envisages all possibilities for the future. 'Christ' is to be thought of therefore as 'creative transformation'. Jesus is the Christ because he brought into history a distinctive structure or existence. Jesus thus revealed the truth about reality so that we may be creatively transformed. He presents to us God's good intention for us, inviting us to yield to the 'lure' of God's love.

This does appear to be a genuine attempt to express the true deity and the true humanity of Christ without using the traditional Hellenistic terminology of the creeds and so dispensing with the metaphysics that they seem to imply. The question has to be raised, however, whether Process Theology as a whole is compatible with Christian faith in the God and Father of our Lord Jesus Christ. If the Process theologians are to be consistent, the human being Jesus cannot be a continuing reality but, like the rest of the human race, has to be re-interpreted as a fleeting series of 'actual occasions'. There is no place therefore for the continuing humanity of Christ and his present priestly intercession before the Father. His death and resurrection, far from being at the centre of the Gospel, are marginalized. It has to be asked whether anything was actually changed when he died and rose again: whether humanity was definitively reconciled to God and salvation accomplished.

Hick: The Myth of Christ

Lastly, in this brief review of the 'Liberal' tradition in Christology we may note the views of John Hick (1922–2012). Experiencing evangelical conversion while a student at Edinburgh, Hick gradually veered away from orthodox Christian faith. When he published his influential textbook on theodicy, *Evil and the God of Love*, he still held to the Incarnation. His theodicy claimed to be 'Irenaean' rather than 'Augustinian', but it was really deeply influenced by Schleiermacher.

By the time he published *God and the Universe of Faiths* in 1973,[5] Hick was advocating a 'Copernican revolution', 'a paradigm shift from a Christianity-centred or Jesus-centred model to a God-centred model.'[6] This was developed further in *God Has Many Names* in 1980. It required a different Christology, for if Jesus Christ was actually God Incarnate, then it was difficult to avoid the conclusion that all must be converted to faith in him. The alternative was to understand the Incarnation 'metaphorically rather than literally, as an essentially poetic expression of the Christian's devotion to his Lord.'[7] Hick had edited a collection of essays advocating such a view, *The Myth of God Incarnate*, a publication that gained considerable notoriety and provoked widespread debate.[8] By the time he gave his Gifford Lectures in 1986-87, Hick had moved from a theocentric model to what he called '*Reality*centredness' in order to accommodate the non-theistic religions.[9]

Perhaps we should see Hick's view of world religions as the *reductio ad absurdum* of modernity's 'Liberal' Theology. The whole tradition from Schleiermacher onward has often tried to give some kind of special place to Jesus Christ, to regard him as superlative in one way or another and so a symbol for 'God'. The Christian 'myth' is rejected along with the 'myths' of all other religions. But in fact as soon as the uniqueness

---

5. John Hick, *God and the Universe of Faiths* (London: Macmillan, 1973).

6. John Hick, *God Has Many Names* (Philadelphia: Westminster, 1980), 18.

7. Hick, 19.

8. John Hick, ed., *The Myth of God Incarnate* (London: SCM, 1977).

9. John Hick, *An Interpretation of Religion: Human Responses to the Transcendent* (New Haven, CT: Yale University Press, 1990).

of Christ is denied or even compromised, as soon as we deny that 'Jesus Christ is Lord' and refuse to accept his identification with God, we end up back with the 'unknown god' of the Athenians in Acts 17. God appears to retreat (as with Kant) into unknowable mystery.

'Liberal' Theology not only fails to be 'liberal' in any meaningful sense of the word other than playing fast and loose with the Christian faith, but it fails to bring us to God. Many who are attracted to it because of its apparent embodiment of Enlightenment ideals try in various ways to give some explanation to the 'deity' of Christ so as to allow them to claim to be Christians. But in the end it proclaims a different gospel. Christians have much to learn from the Enlightenment, but ultimately it is Jesus Christ who is the Light of the world. He alone is the Way, the Truth, and the Life. These are not superlatives but absolutes. Christ alone is the unique Son of the Father in whom God reveals himself by the Spirit and adopts us into his family.

Liberal Theology, with its apologetic motive, aimed to *contextualize* the Christian Gospel in the world of 'modernity', but it ended up again and again with a syncretism that transformed the Gospel of Christ, crucified and risen, truly human and truly God, into another gospel.

EIGHT

Christology Re-expressed

While the ingenious and creative theologians of the 'Liberal' tradition attempted to recast the doctrine of Christ to speak to the philosophies and culture of modernity, many in the Church stayed true to the mainstream Christian tradition. They continued to affirm the Nicene Creed and the substance of the Chalcedonian Symbol, believing them to be reliable interpretations of the teaching of the apostles in inspired Scripture. Arising out of the Evangelical awakening of the eighteenth century, led by Edwards, Whitefield, and the Wesleys, came the great missionary movement of the nineteenth century. This led in turn to the revolution in world Christianity in the twentieth century that sees the vibrant churches of the global South and East today far outnumbering the older churches of Europe and North America.

In this context, we are seeing a return to a Christ-centred Theology and a reaffirmation of faith in Jesus Christ as the only Son of God, who became fully human, died on the cross for our salvation, and rose again. Modernity is said to be giving way to fashionable 'postmodernity', which is, at the very least, a humbler awareness of the overblown claims of 'modern' thought. In this cultural, global context, 'Liberal' Theology and the churches that adhere to it are fading. In this context, it is helpful for us to consider the thinking of some Christian theologians who thought creatively *within* the tradition that affirmed Nicaea and Chalcedon as the valid interpretation of the Christology of the New Testament. We do not necessarily have to agree with everything they said in order to recognize them as working within the living tradition of orthodox Christian belief in Jesus Christ as Lord.

Kierkegaard: Lutheran and Pietist

Although rather an obscure figure during his lifetime, at least outside the kingdom of Denmark, Søren Kierkegaard (1813-55) became influential in the twentieth century. Some have interpreted his language of the 'leap of faith' as advocating existentialism or some form of irrationalism. It has been argued, however, that this is a deeply misguided view. Kierkegaard is not rejecting reason for an irrational form of fideism: rather, he is rejecting 'Reason' with a capital 'R', the proud rationalism of the Enlightenment and later of Hegel.[1]

To understand something of the context, it is important to note that his family were participants in both the established Lutheran Church of Denmark and in a Pietist congregation in the Moravian tradition. Like the Pietists and like Wesley, Kierkegaard therefore came to criticize nominal Christianity. He increasingly reacted against what he saw as the inauthenticity of the Lutheranism of established Danish Christianity. He also rejected the Romantic theology of Schleiermacher, since it appeared to 'reduce religion to an affective, subjective experience.'[2] Neither Hegel nor Schleiermacher had provided an acceptable Christian response to the Enlightenment or its aftermath.

Kierkegaard developed his heritage from Moravian Pietism in a very different way from Schleiermacher. He insisted that 'subjectivity is truth', but this did not mean that he followed Schleiermacher or that he was a relativist who rejected objective reality, particularly the reality of God. He also wrote that 'subjectivity is untruth'! What he appeared to mean was that the meaning of a statement depends on 'who said it, on what occasion, in what situation.'[3] In short, a true statement may be made untruthfully or inauthentically by one who was not really engaging with the reality being spoken about, but merely repeating second-hand notions. This was a false

---

1. See C. Stephen Evans, *Passionate Reason: Making Sense of Kierkegaard's Philosophical Fragments* (Bloomington, IN: Indiana University Press, 1992).

2. See Tim Rose, *Kierkegaard's Christocentric Theology* (Aldershot: Ashgate, 2001), 31.

3. See Lee C. Barrett III, *Kierkegaard* (Nashville: Abingdon, 2010), 17.

objectivity. Particularly when it comes to God, there must be passionate engagement by the speaker, a network of emotions, passions, and attitudes that Kierkegaard referred to as 'pathos', 'inwardness', or 'subjectivity'. False objectivity he called 'direct communication', the reciting of mere information: but to speak of God truly requires the 'indirect communication' of personal involvement.

This is why Kierkegaard is deliberately difficult to read. He demands that the reader wrestle with the text, even giving mixed signals, playing with irony, tensions, paradoxes, incongruities, and using pseudonyms for some of his writings. The reader is not allowed to rest in a system of neutral, apparently objective doctrines, for grasping the Truth requires not just neutral detachment but personal decision and commitment. It is a matter not only of the intellect but of the will. Faith always involves risk.

The Absolute Paradox

Kierkegaard presents the 'absolute paradox' in his work *Philosophical Fragments*. It is important to see that this is one of his pseudonymous works, presented as written by one Johannes Climacus, 'John the Climber'. Climacus is a non-Christian who develops a 'project of thought' starting with the question, raised by Socrates in several of Plato's dialogues, 'How far does the Truth admit of being learned?' More specifically, can virtue be taught? For Socrates, a teacher cannot communicate knowledge or virtue directly to his student; rather, he must play the role of a midwife, helping to bring to birth or to explicit expression what the student already knows implicitly. This was tied to the notion of the eternal existence of the soul: the soul is *recollecting* what it already knew from all eternity.

Writing as Johannes Climacus, Kierkegaard poses alternative hypotheses. Hypothesis A is the Socratic one that discovering the Truth is discovering knowledge that is already deeply immanent within us. Kierkegaard has in mind here not only the Idealism of Hegel but also the thought of Schleiermacher.[4] He may also have had in mind the surviving contemporary schools of Enlightenment rationalism and empiricism.[5] All of these schools of thought arising from the Enlightenment share this 'immanent' assumption of Socrates and Plato that ultimate truth lies within the soul or is accessible to the human mind.

Hypothesis B, as it is developed in the *Philosophical Fragments* by 'Climacus', is therefore actually 'an incarnational theology of revelation'. Writing under the pseudonym of the non-Christian Climacus, Kierkegaard omits traditional Christological terminology. For 'Climacus' it is merely a 'project of thought', a hypothesis. The Teacher must bring to the seeker not only the Truth but also the condition for understanding it. Since the learner does not have the Truth within himself, he must be transformed; he must be 'born again'; he must become a 'new creature'. The Teacher is the Unknown, that is to say: God.

God's resolve to do this must be moved by love and must be from eternity, 'though when realized in time it constitutes precisely the *Moment*.' This love leads to a deep grief felt by God alone, for God alone understands the misunderstanding. A king who loves a humble maiden will not simply dazzle her with his splendour, nor simply raise her to his side where she would be devastated by such sudden prominence. He must come down to her: he must take 'the form of a servant'. For God, this could not be assumed simply as an outer garment. He must take our very humanity in all its suffering and mortality. This, according to Climacus, is the 'Absolute Paradox'.

That Kierkegaard regarded the Incarnation as a 'paradox' has been interpreted by many as embracing irrationality. But the word may refer to a rhetorical figure, an *apparent* absurdity or contradiction that actually captures a hidden truth. The paradox is therefore not to be understood as a logical contradiction between time and eternity, defined as timelessness. The 'qualitative difference' is not merely between the infinite and the finite, but between God and *the sinner*.

---

4. Evans, *Passionate Reason*, 29-31.

5. Rose, *Kierkegaard's Christocentric Theology*, 39.

Kierkegaard's gospel of the Incarnation as the unique way of Atonement or reconciliation therefore contrasts with Schleiermacher's view of Christ as superlative, as the best mediator (so far), and with the Enlightenment view (as expressed by Lessing) that 'the contingent truths of history can never become the demonstration of necessary truths of reason.' That was Lessing's 'ugly, broad ditch'. Lessing's Enlightenment scepticism and the attempted responses of Schleiermacher and Hegel were all 'Socratic' as far as Kierkegaard was concerned. They all assumed a fundamental continuity between eternal divinity and the human soul so that no real event or change was possible or even necessary. All that was required was deeper understanding.

Kierkegaard had perceptively put his finger on what was later to be called 'the scandal of particularity'. It is at this point that the Christian proclamation of the Incarnation, that God became human in Jesus Christ, is in conflict with the whole Socratic, Hellenistic philosophical tradition even in its modern guise. Real sin, real rebellion, a real hostility between God and humanity, could not be thought away by deeper appreciation of eternal truths. It has to be *done* away in the cross of Christ. Right at the heart of Kierkegaard's Theology therefore is what he called a 'paradox', but which the Fathers more often referred to as the 'mystery' of Christ.[6]

Forsyth: Rejecting Liberalism

P.T. Forsyth (1848–1921) was a Scottish Congregationalist whose gift for striking paradoxes alerts us, as Kierkegaard did, to the mystery and centrality of the Incarnation. He studied for a year in Germany with Albrecht Ritschl but later rejected Liberal Theology and returned to Evangelical Theology, emphasizing the centrality of the cross of Christ as the objective redemption of humanity. Forsyth's clear vision saw that the Liberal Theology of his day was essentially anthropocentric: God and Christ were treated as means to an end, namely, the perfecting of humanity. He rejected the Liberal

---

6. See Rose, 65-78.

tendency to replace the centrality of the Person of Christ with the preaching of the kingdom of God. 'To bring the kingdom,' he retorted, 'preach the King.'[7] Forsyth rejected scathingly a Liberalism that was little more than an expression of nineteenth-century Romanticism in its emphasis on the love of God to the rejection of the New Testament's clear warnings about his wrath. This resulted in a resurgent Pelagianism.

But Forsyth had little time for the 'metaphysical' language of classical Christology, particularly the language of 'two natures'. With the growth of modern Psychology, he thought, 'such formulae were bound to dissolve.'[8] But while the metaphysical language of 'two natures' should not be retained, the Incarnation was essential to Christian faith, particularly the personal faith of the Reformation. This required what he calls 'the finality of Christ', for in Christianity (unlike Hegelianism), the Absolute is not an idea but an experience of the historic and most human Christ as 'the one moral mediator of personal communion with the living, and holy, and eternal God.' Christ is not *a* revelation of God: he is *the* revelation.[9]

The 'finality' of Christ and the cruciality of the cross therefore demand the pre-existence of Christ. If his relation with the Father only began within time, then his sacrifice is only that of a great martyr. The Christological hymn of Philippians 2 is crucial, for if his cross is of universal, cosmic significance, then it must be the outcome not just of Christ's earthly life but of a commitment made in eternity. This is not just a matter of satisfying some philosophical theme or theological dogma. It was essential for our salvation. The act of self-renunciation must be that of a Saviour who is not just a man and not merely a 'middle being who was a mere emanation from God in a world process.'[10] It must be the loving act of God. It is not enough that the cross works subjectively in us to elicit

---

7. Peter T. Forsyth, *The Person and Place of Jesus Christ* (London: Hodder and Stoughton, 1909), 123.

8. Forsyth, 217.

9. Forsyth, 251-52.

10. Forsyth, 277-78.

faith and love: to have objective, eternal consequences, it must be the act of God.

Christ and Kenosis

But insisting on the full deity of Christ raises a problem: 'If we hold to the personal pre-existence of Christ, do we not render His life as the historical Jesus unreal? . . . Could a pre-existent Christ be a real man?'[11] This question leads Forsyth to develop his doctrine of the *kenōsis*. If we do not advocate *krypsis*, the mere 'hiding' of the divine powers in the man Jesus resulting in a kind of play-acting, then we need some doctrine of *kenōsis*, self-emptying.

Forsyth then applies this real restriction in Jesus' knowledge to the question of his sinlessness. He maintains the strong view that not only did he not sin, but he could not sin. This may appear to be contrary to his genuine humanity. If it was impossible for him to sin, how could his temptations be real? Was this not play-acting? Forsyth makes a suggestion: that although it was impossible for him to sin, he did not know that. Each temptation was therefore a genuine battle and a genuine victory. Forsyth brought the question home to his listeners by posing the question whether they could steal something from a shop on their way home. In one sense, that would be quite possible, but in another, quite impossible!

Some kenoticists had distinguished between the 'relative' attributes of God consequent upon his creation of the world, namely, his omniscience, omnipotence, and omnipresence, and his 'immanent' attributes, namely, the ethical or spiritual qualities of love and grace. The former were said to be renounced in the *kenōsis*, but not the latter. But Forsyth is not happy with that. He prefers to think of 'two modes of being'. The attributes of God, he argues, are not destroyed when they are reduced to a potentiality. 'Self-reduction' or 'self-retraction' might be a better phrase than 'self-emptying'.

Like Kierkegaard, Forsyth stood in the Evangelical tradition of the Reformation. Reacting against the Liberalism of the Ritschlian school, he nonetheless shared the concern

---

11. Forsyth, 289.

of modernity with the true humanity of Christ. Dispensing with the technical metaphysical terminology of Chalcedon, he nevertheless held to the true deity of the Nicene faith but tried to enter into a deeper understanding of the true humanity. To do so, he advocated a certain measured use of a kenotic Christology.

Brunner: Liberalism and 'Religion'

Karl Barth and Emil Brunner were the leading figures, as we have seen, in the reaction against Liberal Theology referred to as 'the Theology of the Word', or sometimes as 'Dialectical Theology'. While Bultmann became strongly influenced by existentialism and led a new phase of a quite different Liberal Theology, Barth and Brunner both affirmed the Christology of Nicaea and Chalcedon as true to the Christology of the New Testament.

Emil Brunner (1889–1966), professor of Theology at Zürich, presented his formulation of the centrality of Christ in his 1927 work, *The Mediator*.[12] Like the Christology of Kierkegaard, this was not so much a close examination of the technical vocabulary of Chalcedon, nor an attempt to wrestle with the paradox of the One who was both God and human. It was more an exploration of why Incarnation and Atonement had to be at the heart of Christian Theology and why this focus on Christ was the only possible and effective response to the epistemological questions and the increasingly influential scepticism of modernity.

Brunner begins *The Mediator* with the assertion that all religion claims to come from revelation. For the various traditional popular religions, these were oracles, theophanies, and myths. But for modern, educated Europeans, following in the Hellenistic philosophical tradition, these differences between religions were accidental and there was really only one religion. It derived from inner mystical revelation, and this was timeless and universal. With Ritschl, this was some-

---

12. Published in German, citations herein are from the English translation: Emil Brunner, *The Mediator: A Study of the Central Doctrine of the Christian Faith*, trans. Olive Wyon (London: Lutterworth, 1934).

what different. He rejected the metaphysical for the moral, but in fact his system was dominated by the idea of God as Love. The kingdom of God was therefore a movement in history for common human action from the motive of love.

In contrast to that, Brunner insisted that Christian faith was not just one example of general 'religion' arising from a general revelation accessible to all in the depth of their own souls. Rather, it is centred upon the once-for-all historical event that it affirms to be the unique and final revelation of God, the Incarnation. For Brunner, the modern Liberal Theologies of Schleiermacher, Hegel, and Ritschl failed to escape the assumption that there was a common 'essence of religion' which all religions shared.

Brunner analyzed this as a failure to grasp the reality of evil. For all of these streams of Liberal Theology there was an unbroken continuity between the human and the divine. Liberal Theology believed that our reason and science or our mystical contemplation or our moral will could bring us to Ultimate Truth. From this came the myth of progress and the easy optimism of self-sufficiency. Liberal Theology was Pelagian. In contrast to that, the authentic Christian faith alone perceived the reality of the breakdown in relationship, the great gulf between God and humanity, namely, the reality of evil.

While the historian can therefore establish the historicity of Christ 'after the flesh', history, given its own understanding of its methodology, cannot cope with the unique entry of the Eternal into time.[13] Christian faith does not arise therefore out of the historian's interpretation of historical evidence, but only out of the preached and written witness of the apostles and prophets, that is, from the Holy Scriptures.

Christ the Mediator

This brings Brunner to Christology proper, beginning with 'The Divine Word'. The Greeks rightly thought of the Logos as giving structure to the universe and as absolutely necessary for intelligent thought, including moral as well as physical law. Yet this cannot be merely a principle or an Idea,

---

13. Brunner, chap. 6.

but must be a 'personal communication', a real 'Thou', if there is to be personal relationship, conversation, and responsibility. Knowledge of the real personal God can only come through a personal self-communication, an event that is not part of the historical process, but absolutely unique.[14] The Word of the Lord spoken by the prophet was never something that could be deduced from what we already know. It could only be believed. But the prophets pointed to One who was 'more than a prophet', for here alone 'Word' and 'Person' are identical.

Christology, confessing Jesus Christ the Mediator, is therefore the centre and foundation of the Christian religion. It addresses two inseparable questions: 'Who is he?' and, given that he is the divine Word, 'What does God have to say to us in him?' This brings Brunner to the Chalcedonian terminology of 'two natures' and specifically to 'divine nature' as the phrase that asserts his true deity. The answer to, 'Who is he?' is that he is God. As the Word, he is not just an intellectual message, but his coming means that *God himself* has crossed the gulf, 'transcending the frontier between the creature and the Creator from the side of God.'[15]

But in speaking of his divine 'Person', we must not confuse that with 'personality'. 'Personality, in our human, historical sense of the word, belongs to the humanity of the Son of God, not to His deity.'[16] His 'Person' is the *incognito* of his deity, which cannot be known by the method of History. Curiously, those who reject the language of 'nature' as impersonal, but then proceed to speak of him as the 'Bearer of the Word' (he is thinking of Bultmann), thereby divide 'person' from 'idea'. And 'idea' always claims supremacy over 'person' as that which is essential and eternal. Here alone then all subordination of 'person' to 'idea' ceases, for this Logos is not an 'idea', but a 'person'. And a person can only be received and known by faith. That which is revealed is therefore the Reveal-

---

14. Brunner, 212.
15. Brunner, 242.
16. Brunner, 266.

er. 'He Himself, not only His message or His Gospel, is from above.' In fact, 'The Christ who came *is* the Gospel.'[17]

This brings Brunner to 'the fact of the Incarnation'.[18] 'The central truth of the Christian faith is this: that the eternal Son of God took upon Himself our humanity, not that the man Jesus acquired divinity.' He quotes a key sentence from Luther: 'He assumed what is ours in order to confer on us what is his.'[19] The Logos assumed human nature so that his human life is fully human and historical. To speak of his human mind (*nous*) is to say that he had a fully human personality with its own psychology, but he is not a human 'Person'. He is a Person who has become human. Brunner distinguishes this technical Trinitarian term, 'person', from the psychological meaning of the word 'personality'. Jesus has a human personality, since he has a human mind (*nous*): but he was not a human mind or personality in eternity. He acquired that at his Incarnation.

By assuming the whole human nature, he has entered into solidarity with the whole human race, but this only profits those who believe. The 'significance of the humanity of Christ' is therefore that the self-manifestation of God is at the same time a veiling.[20] The revealing encounter is therefore 'indirect'. Direct communication would mean the passive transfer of knowledge: but that it is veiled and so 'indirect' means that God does not force himself upon us. We are each summoned therefore to a real decision, the 'leap of faith'.

Barth: The Word Made Flesh

Karl Barth (1886–1968) and Emil Brunner were very close in seeing Christology as central to Christian Theology. That was despite their disagreement in 1934 when Barth denounced Brunner's attempt to find a subsidiary place for 'Natural Theology'. Barth's Christology and its implications

---

17. Brunner, 272.

18. Brunner, chap. 12.

19. See Brunner, 316. Brunner quotes the Latin version: *Nostra assumsit ut conferret nobis sua.*

20. Brunner, chap. 13.

for all of Christian Theology was worked out in his massive *Church Dogmatics*, published in German from 1932 to 1967. We shall confine ourselves here to his first articulation of the doctrine of Christ in the first volume, particularly section 15, entitled 'The Mystery of Revelation'.[21]

Barth first introduces 'The Problem of Christology'. The reality of revelation, to which the Old and New Testaments witness, is the Easter story and message. That is to say that revelation comes in the resurrection of Jesus Christ which reveals his hidden work in his passion, including within that, his whole life on earth. Christian Theology must be Christologically determined or it succumbs to some alien sway. Therefore, Christology, addressing the question, 'Who is Jesus Christ?' is basic. The content of this 'express doctrine' is the Incarnation, 'God and man becoming one in Jesus Christ.' There is no higher or prior vantage point or presupposition from which Christian Theology can begin.

Jesus Christ is 'Very God and Very Man', and Barth's treatment of this is an exposition of John 1:14, 'The Word became flesh.' The Word is the divine, creative, reconciling, redeeming Word, the eternal Son of God. Jesus Christ, who is identified with this Word, is therefore the one, true, eternal God, the Lord of heaven and earth. Barth notes that 'the Word' is the subject of this sentence, 'The Word became flesh.' Nothing befalls him: he acts in a sovereign divine act that is like the act of creation yet different from it. This is not a world-process (against Hegelianism), but an act of divine freedom, and even in becoming what he was not before, the Word remains the free, sovereign Word of God. 'Very God and Very Man' therefore indicates an equation, 'but strictly speaking, this equation is irreversible.' It has pleased very God to become very man, not *vice versa*. The Word remains what he was before becoming flesh, and in becoming flesh he never ceases to be the Word.

---

21. Karl Barth, *Church Dogmatics*, vol. I, *The Doctrine of the Word of God,* pt. 2, sec. 15, trans. G.T. Thomson and Harold Knight, ed. G.W. Bromiley and T.F. Torrance (London: T&T Clark, 1956), 122-202.

The word 'flesh' implies 'human essence and existence', not an already existing human being. It is not as if there were first a man there so that the Son of God became that man. Rather, this man came into being when the Word became flesh: he is not a second kind of being in Jesus Christ alongside the Son of God. Therefore: 'God Himself in person is the Subject of a real human being and acting.'[22] 'Flesh' also means that the Word assumes our human existence 'in the state and position, amid the conditions, under the curse and punishment of sinful man.'[23] Otherwise he would not touch *us* and his action would not be a revealing and reconciling action. But: 'Our unholy human existence, assumed and adopted by the Word of God, is a hallowed and therefore a sinless existence.'[24]

The verb in the text, 'became', refers to an act of the Word, for humanity has no capacity to become the humanity of the Word. The paraphrase 'The Word assumed flesh' guards against the misinterpretation that the Word ceases to be the Word of God in the full sense. It also guards against another misinterpretation, that in the union of divine and human being and nature a third thing arises. Jesus Christ is the Mediator between God and Man, but not midway between the two. He is the God-man, fully God and fully man. The event to which this verb, 'became,' refers must be understood as a *completed* event, an accomplished, objective fact. But it must also be understood as a completed *event*: that is to say that it is true because it *became* true. In the vision of faith, the act is repeated. We envisage the division between God and humanity in order that the unity may be seen as an *act* of God. Barth concludes that there is a riddle in the fact itself.

The Miracle of Christmas

The third subsection of 'The Mystery of Revelation' is entitled 'The Miracle of Christmas', and here Barth addresses the doctrine of the virgin birth. This doctrine, explicitly affirmed in the Nicene Creed, had been dismissed by Liberal

22. Barth, vol. I, pt. 2, sec. 15, p. 151.
23. Barth, vol. I, pt. 2, sec. 15, p. 155.
24. Barth, vol. I, pt. 2, sec. 15, p. 156.

theologians on the historical-critical grounds that it is not mentioned in the earlier books of the New Testament but only in two of the Gospels. It also ran counter to the general dismissal of miracles by the 'modern' mind. It was particularly dismissed because of the standard Augustinian interpretation linking it to the negative attitude to human sexuality. Even Brunner had dismissed the virgin birth as a primitive attempt at a 'biological explanation' of the Incarnation. Running completely contrary to this twentieth-century consensus, Barth astounded his contemporaries by affirming the doctrine.

It was important to see that this was not merely a repetition of the doctrine of the Incarnation, nor a primitive biological explanation. It was related to the Incarnation as the *sign* to the thing *signified*, as the *form* inseparable from the *content*. To reject the *sign* was to reject the thing *signified*, for what it indicates is that in revelation and reconciliation, *the initiative lies wholly with God*. As a *sign*, this *miracle* of Christmas is analogous to the *mystery* of Christmas that it signifies.

It was this Chalcedonian doctrine of Christ, carefully balancing the emphases of the Alexandrians and Antiochenes, that Barth worked with in the succeeding volumes of his *Church Dogmatics*. In his fourth volume, he wrote at great length to show how this doctrine was at the core of the Christian understanding of salvation. His massive work continues to stimulate discussion and debate and marks the beginning of a new era in Christian Theology. But it is clear that, whatever we may make of his Theology as a whole, his starting point is the doctrine of Christ formulated by the Christian Fathers as the Church's interpretation of the New Testament.

The consideration of Christology, the Church's teaching about Jesus Christ, did not end with Karl Barth.

The survey of these four giants of Christian thought in this chapter brings us therefore to consider the questions that have faced Christian believers all through the centuries as they have proclaimed that Jesus Christ is Lord.

Christ: God and Human

We have been pursuing the question, 'Who is Jesus Christ?' and we need now to recap, to retrace briefly the road we have come.

Prelude: Learning from Historical Research

First, we examined the attempt made by historians to provide an answer. We noted that the historical-critical method does provide more positive conclusions than were reached fifty or sixty years ago, and that is not likely to be reversed. The historian can confirm that this man lived, that he was an itinerant prophet with a band of disciples, and that he proclaimed the coming of God's kingdom. Many historians also agree that he claimed to be the Christ or Messiah but that he redefined that role by choosing to go to his death. There is widespread agreement, too, that his challenge to the priestly cast in the temple and the new interpretation he gave to the Passover meal in the Last Supper were indications of why he chose to die.

But the historical-critical method is stumped by the empty tomb and the accounts of his resurrection. There is no credible alternative historical explanation of what happened other than his resurrection. This challenges us to abandon the deistic or atheistic limits we place on what can happen. We are challenged to see the God of Israel, at work in a hidden way through the long centuries, now at work in Jesus' bodily resurrection from the dead.

Historical research thus brings us to the threshold of faith, but it is only by the Spirit that we accept this revolution in our whole way of thinking. It is a paradigm shift, a repentance or conversion of mind, soul, body—our whole being. It is by the Spirit that we are enabled to recognize this man as God Incarnate and to proclaim in faith, 'My Lord and my God!' Only then are we able to articulate our knowledge as 'faith seeking understanding'.

Having come this far in the Prelude—Chapters 1 and 2, we then examined in the four chapters of Part I the witness to Christ in the New Testament and the development arising out of that in the Christian Fathers.

Part I: Scripture and Tradition

In Chapter 3, it was the Lord's appointed witnesses to his death and resurrection, the apostles, who showed us the way. We began then with the apostolic Gospel, preached in the twenty-year period between the resurrection of the Lord and the penning of one of the earliest writings we have in the New Testament. There in 1 Corinthians we find the summary of the Gospel handed on to Paul by the first apostles after he had met the risen Lord for himself:

> That [he] died for our sins in accordance with the scriptures, that he was buried, that he was raised on the third day in accordance with the scriptures, that he appeared to Cephas, then to the twelve. (15:3-5)

There is the narrative of the apostolic Gospel, first preached by Peter on the day of Pentecost and reflected in the apostles' sermons in the book of Acts. It is one narrative with two episodes about one Person who was crucified and then raised from the dead.

That is the narrative further developed in the Christological hymns, in the parabolic shape best seen in Philippians 2:5-11. There the narrative is extended at both ends to begin with the Incarnation of the one who was 'in the form of God' (v. 6) and who is now exalted at the end to participate in God's universal rule. This is the shape of the narrative of the four Gospels and which underlies all the writings of the New Testament. It is this one-in-two Gospel narrative that provides us with the hermeneutic for interpreting not only the apostolic writings of the New Testament but all the books of the Hebrew Bible, which we now call the Old Testament.

It is this one-in-two shape of the Gospel that gives us the one-in-two shape of the Church's declaration of faith in Christ. It is this Gospel that reveals to us his true and full humanity in his life, obedient to death, and that reveals to us in his resurrection his true and full deity as God the Son, the very source of eternal life.

In Chapters 4 and 5, we saw that it is this one-in-two shape of the One who is truly human and truly God that was defended by the earliest bishops, developed by Irenaeus, and defended by Athanasius. It is this one-in-two doctrine of Christ that was affirmed in the second article of the Nicene Creed, reflecting the shape of the hymn of Philippians 2, and further defended in the Chalcedonian Symbol. These documents employ Hellenistic language and categories to contextualize the core of the Christian faith, but they faithfully represent the one-in-two shape. In Chapter 6, we traced the loyalty to this one-in-two doctrine of Christ in the Evangelical Reformers and their heirs, particularly in the Wesleyan tradition.

Part II: Christ Our Contemporary

It is this New Testament shape of the answer to the question, 'Who is Jesus Christ?' that was defended throughout the centuries of the Church, but challenged again by the modern European culture that developed from its roots in ancient Hellenism. In Chapter 7, we briefly reviewed the major creative Liberal theologians who attempted a fresh contextualization in the aftermath of the Enlightenment but who all too often syncretized the Gospel, conforming it to the vaunted 'modern' culture. We also briefly reviewed in Chapter 8 some of those who saw that and who have tried to re-express the Nicene-Chalcedonian interpretation of the New Testament doctrine. Now in this chapter, we shall take into account more recent writing as we attempt to wrestle with the contemporary questions that arise.

Only now that we have followed the conversation so far through Historical Theology are we sufficiently informed to engage with the issues in the conversation today. In this chapter therefore, we will concentrate on the 'two'—true deity and true humanity. In the final chapter, we shall concentrate on the one Person, our Lord Jesus Christ.

Truly God: The Offence of the Gospel

As we have seen, Jesus, who was recognized during his earthly life as 'Messiah' or 'Christ', was now openly declared after his resurrection to be 'Lord' and 'God' and consequently *worshipped*. That changed everything. It was not that the faith of Israel was repudiated. Quite the contrary: the faith of Israel was held to be fulfilled. The Church still worshipped the One God, the God of Abraham, Isaac, and Jacob, the I AM who revealed himself to Moses and who was declared to be One in Israel's great declaration, the *Shema*: 'Hear, O Israel: The LORD our God, the LORD is one' (Deut. 6:4, NIV). But they now included the *Lord* Jesus Christ *within* the one God whom they worshipped.

In our contemporary context, it is the one-in-two Gospel, and particularly the deity of Christ, the confession that Jesus Christ is *Lord*, that distinguishes the Christian faith from all that is opposed to it and from all that only seems to be Christian. The exclusiveness of the worship of Old Israel therefore carries over into the exclusiveness in the Christian faith today. That is of course offensive. Was the hallmark of the ministry of Jesus not his *inclusiveness*? Are exclusiveness and discrimination not the great evils against which our 'enlightened' modern or postmodern civilization rightly reacts? Are these not offensive in the light of the great modern principles, the gods of Liberty, Equality, and Fraternity? Should we not then in the name of peace and tolerance and civilization moderate our claims and agree that Jesus is only one way of many ways to God?

There is of course a great deal that we must say strongly and uncompromisingly in favour of tolerance, equality, and inclusiveness. Tertullian declared, 'It is assuredly no part of religion to compel religion.'[1] After Constantine, the Christian

---

1. Tertullian, 'To Scapula', chap. 2, in vol. 3 of *Ante-Nicene Fathers*, ed. Alexander Roberts and James Donaldson (1885; repr., Peabody, MA: Hendrickson, 1994), 105.

Church was too often seduced into the notion that the power of the state should be used to compel conformity to the Christian establishment. But tolerance is a civic virtue that does not mean indifference to the truth. Christians surely ought to uphold freedom of religion and freedom of speech and the equality of all religions before the civil law. But the whole point of tolerance is to permit disagreement, and the confession of Jesus Christ as Lord is the point at which Christians have to disagree with other faiths.

Dialogue with the great world religions with their rich cultures of literature and spirituality ought to be conducted in mutual tolerance and, indeed, the highest mutual respect. But to do so, it must be *honest* dialogue that recognizes that each of the world faiths claims to be the right and true faith. The claim to a unique grasp of the truth also characterizes the faith or ideology or 'life-stance' of Secular Humanism. Despite their championing of tolerance and inclusiveness, Secular Humanists claim that they are right (and therefore the great world religions wrong) in denying the existence of any reality that cannot be apprehended by the five senses. And secularism increasingly tends to claim precedence, even showing a degree of intolerance, at least in the Western nations.

The Inclusive Saviour

However, it also has to be said that it is certainly part of Christian faith that this universal Lord is also the *inclusive* Saviour who summons *all* to faith and obedience. Apart from one minority tradition, all Christians proclaim with the New Testament that Christ died *for all*. The ministry of Jesus reveals the universal love of God *for all*, particularly the poor and oppressed and marginalized. There is no need for any to perish at the coming Last Judgment: 'All may live, for Christ has died.' But the same inclusive Lord will resist and condemn all the evil that brings suffering to his creatures, and that means that he will reject and exclude those who persist in their selfish ways and intentionally reject him.

It is at this point sadly that the great modern tradition of 'Liberal' Christianity fails. Moved by the apologetic motive to contextualize Christian faith in Western culture in the aftermath of the Enlightenment, it was never quite sufficiently clear on the deity of Christ and sometimes even denied him. It has been characterized by 'degree Christology', using superlatives about Christ that never quite amounted to an exclusive claim to *uniqueness*. But to use only superlatives for Christ is to dishonour him. Here in Christ *alone* God has become human: here *alone* God the Son became the Lamb who bore away the sin of the world: here *alone* God is finally and definitively revealed by his Spirit in his incarnate Son. At the very heart of the Christian faith is the *solus Christus*, the claim to the *uniqueness* of the Lord Jesus Christ as the *only* Son of the Father, and so the *only* human being who is to be worshipped as Lord and God.

It is the fact that our Lord Jesus Christ shares in the uniqueness of God which makes Christian Theology such an odd form of discourse among the academic disciplines of today's secular universities. Human logic, certainly in the Western tradition stemming from Aristotle, operates by classification into categories. The problem is then how this whole way of thinking, devised to deal with the space-time world we inhabit, can cope with the unique One who is declared to be the transcendent Creator of the space-time world. Can this Creator Lord God also be included within our creaturely categories, even if only by consigning him to a category of one?

The problem is seen to be an inevitable part of Christology as soon as we identify Jesus Christ as *Lord*, and therefore as one with the Father in the unity of the Holy Spirit. The uniqueness of God means that God cannot be reduced to finite categories, but here in Christology the problem is compounded. This One is said to be simultaneously unique as God, but also, as one of us, a particular human being within the space-time world. As a human being, he is within a category, subject to finite logic. He is also subject to causality within the space-time world. But as God, he is not. Using Gabriel Marcel's distinction, we have to classify this, therefore, not as merely a 'problem', which is in principle soluble, but as a 'mystery'. It is in fact *the* Mystery, 'the mystery of godliness' (1 Tim. 3:16, KJV).

That does not mean to say that there is no logic in Christology and that we may proclaim whatever illogical nonsense we please. A logical system like that of Aristotle is partly applicable because we are speaking of One who is truly human. But the overall logic to which we are committed as Christians is the logic of the narrative of the Christian Gospel, definitively laid out for us, for example, in the Christological hymn of Philippians 2:6-11 and in the second article of the Nicene Creed, further explicated (despite its limitations) in the Chalcedonian Symbol.

Truly Human: The True Humanism

If 'Liberal' or modernist theology failed to be clear on the full *deity* of Christ, believers in the orthodox Nicene and Evangelical tradition of the Reformation can often neglect the significance of the true *humanity* of Christ. The most subtle form of this is Apollinarianism, which accepts the physical reality of his human body but fails to take into account his truly human mind. Many have never fully grasped the historic doctrine of the Church, that Jesus truly thought as a human being with an understanding that developed in a truly human way.

Here it is useful to note that 'humanism' began, not with today's Secular Humanists, but with the Christian humanism of the Renaissance, shared by Reformers such as Zwingli, Calvin, and Cranmer. This led to the flourishing of the humanities—the 'arts'. It has been argued that Christianity is the only true humanism, and humanism in modern times certainly had its genesis within Christian culture and civilization. The very claim that the Eternal God became a *human* being gives humanity a pivotal dignity in the universe, despite being dwarfed by its immensity. The danger of an anthropocentric focus, however, displacing the worship of the Lord God with the celebration and even the worship of humanity, has been with us since the first temptation 'to be as gods'.

Secular Humanism, despite the small membership of Secularist and Humanist societies, has become all-pervasive as the plausibility structure in Western culture today. Christians must not react to this by denigrating humanity, and a truly Christian humanism can find its foundation in the humanity of Christ. The key question then at this point is how we give due weight to the true *humanity* of Christ without thereby compromising his *deity*.

Much Christian Theology since Renaissance humanism burst upon the scene has focused on *the human*. The doctrine of humanity ('theological anthropology') fascinates us. In the doctrine of Christ, we noted that focusing on the human was characteristic of the classic Liberal Theology, closely allied to the first quest for the historical Jesus. Whereas that failed to rise above a 'degree' Christology to an affirmation of his unique deity, the same charge cannot be laid against the kenoticists of the same period. Kenoticists such as P.T. Forsyth affirmed the full deity of Christ. But the notion that the Son of God somehow emptied himself of some of the attributes of deity, or at least put them on hold at his Incarnation, seems to be trying to gain a fuller vision of his *humanity*.

According to the kenoticists (and Irenaeus), it was the *human* choices and the *human* faith and obedience of Jesus that won his victory and exaltation. And kenoticism certainly stands out against the impossible notion that the babe lying in the manger, being God, could comprehend all the elements of quantum physics and the theory of relativity. Whatever the theological difficulties of kenoticism, thinking of the attributes of deity as laid aside certainly helps us to imagine how Jesus 'increased in wisdom' (Luke 2:52) like any other *human* child. It is easier in that way to imagine the Irenaean picture of his developmental sanctification of our humanity at each stage of maturation.

This has been called the 'psychological model' of Christology.[2] It can be seen as having its modern origin in Schleiermacher's concern with the piety of Jesus, his own 'religious' experience of God. The quests for the 'historical' Jesus can also be seen as a pursuit of this 'psychological model'. This may be why the 'quest' for the so-called historical Jesus refuses to die but keeps turning up in a new form! Both the disciplines of History and Psychology focus on the human, and the historical method is not just a matter of chronicling external

---

2. John McIntyre, *The Shape of Christology: Studies in the Doctrine of the Person of Christ*, 2nd ed. (Edinburgh: T&T Clark, 1998), 115ff.

'facts', but of inquiring into the 'inside' of events, the thinking and intention of the human agents. And when we turn to the third quest for the historical Jesus with its much more positive evaluation of the historicity of the evidence, this can certainly help us to do justice to the *humanity* of Christ without denying or compromising his deity. We particularly focused on the reconstruction of the human life and thinking of Jesus by N.T. Wright as particularly helpful.[3]

The 'psychological model' can also be seen in the kind of expository preaching that reconstructs the motives and actions of those who meet Jesus in such a way that the congregation is drawn into the dialogue and engage with Jesus so that they, too, are 'confronted, challenged, judged, forgiven.'[4]

Contextual Christologies: Latin America

The concern with the true humanity of Jesus is also to be seen in the 'contextual' Christologies around the world today. The leading example is the development of Liberation Theology in late twentieth-century Latin America. Concern for the poor, trapped in economic structures producing extremes of wealth and poverty, led to the aim of developing 'base communities' that rooted their theology in *praxis*, practical action, and rejected the reduction of Christian faith to private religious exercises. The point of theology (in a phrase echoing Karl Marx) was 'not to explain the world, but to change it'. This called for a Christological focus on the historical Jesus and his ministry to the poor.

Latin American Evangelical theologians generally accept the view of Liberation Theology that traditional Christology has sometimes so stressed the deity of Christ that the mission of the Church has been severely weakened by failure to emphasize his true humanity. They saw the reaction of Liberation Theology against the complicity of the Roman Catholic Church with serious injustice as fully justified. But on the other hand, the message of Christ could not be *reduced* to issues of social justice highlighted by Marxism. In contrast to

---

3. See Chapter 2, pp. 32ff., esp. pp. 36ff.
4. McIntyre, *Shape of Christology*, 129.

Liberation theologians, they have asserted that our doctrine of Christ must come primarily not from our context but from the biblical revelation. Building on the work of the Scottish missionary and theologian John Mackay in his classic work *The Other Spanish Christ*, Evangelical theologians such a René Padilla, Samuel Escobar, Emilio Antonio Núñez, and Orlando Costas have tried to develop 'a biblically orthodox Christology which would effectively relate to the Latin American reality.'[5]

The same concern with equality and liberty is also reflected in the focus of other contextual Christologies on the humanity of Jesus. Black Christology may have arisen geographically in the West among African Americans, but like Liberation Christology, it focuses on the theme of liberation. According to James Cone, Black Theology arose from the experience of black people in a world of white oppression and exploitation, but also from the revelation that comes to us through Scripture and is appropriated in tradition.[6]

Contextual Christologies: Africa and Asia

African Theology is somewhat different. While postcolonial liberation has been a major theme, there is also the issue of inculturation. When it comes specifically to Christology, John Onaiyekan states: 'If it is true that Christology is at the heart of all Christian Theology, it is particularly true for African Christian Theology.'[7] Veli-Matti Kärkkäinen notes that whereas the study of the Christological titles has been marginalized in the West, it remains significant in Africa. The strong appeal of the *Christus Victor* view of the Atonement in the context of the African search for power means that titles such as 'Son of God', 'Redeemer', and 'Lord' are significant. Other titles drawn from African culture resonate, particularly 'Chief' in Bantu cultures, or 'Healer'. Perhaps the most discussed title

---

5. Sharon E. Heaney, *Contextual Theology for Latin America: Liberation Themes in Evangelical Perspective* (Carlisle, UK: Paternoster, 2008), 161.

6. James Cone, *A Black Theology of Liberation* (Maryknoll, NY: Orbis, 1986).

7. Quoted in Veli-Matti Kärkkäinen, *Christ and Reconciliation*, vol. 1 of *A Constructive Christian Theology for the Pluralistic World* (Grand Rapids: Eerdmans, 2013), 72.

for Christ throughout Africa is the title of 'Ancestor',[8] but it is controversial. While it may be attractive within the Roman Catholic tradition given the practice of praying to the saints, it has not found acceptance generally. It may encourage the notion of the ancestors generally as mediators, reducing Christ to one among many, and that would be contrary to the biblical rejection of necromancy. It may lead, despite the care taken by its advocates, to syncretism.[9]

The Asian context is much more varied. Broadly, we may think of the world of Islam in western Asia, the ancient Hindu traditions of the Indian subcontinent, the Buddhist world of the south-east, and the radically different world of Chinese Confucianism in the far east into which atheistic Western Marxism has brought its own very different worldview. Each of these (not to mention Zoroastrianism, the Sikh religion, Jainism, Taoism, Shinto, and others) has its own challenges for Christians trying to articulate the doctrine of Christ in each of these varied contexts, particularly in thinking about Christ's true humanity. The vastness and variety of the Asian scene is such that we can only begin to suggest here how the *humanity* of Christ is vitally important to Christology in each context.

In the world of Islam in western Asia, the humanity of Christ is common ground and it is his deity that is the flashpoint of disputes that may bring charges of blasphemy. Particularly sensitive in Muslim culture is the understanding of deity, especially the misunderstanding of the Christian doctrine that God generates or begets a Son.

In the Hindu culture of India with its many sophisticated ancient traditions and scriptures, Christ may be *an* incarnation of the divine, but certainly not unique. The Roman Catholic theologian Raimundo Panikkar (1918–2010) revised his book *The Unknown Christ of Hinduism* (1964) in 1981 to move toward a syncretistic version of Christology. Jesus was

8. Kärkkäinen, 77.

9. See Rodney Reed and Gift Mtukwa, 'Christ Our Ancestor: African Christology and the Danger of Contextualization', *Wesleyan Theological Journal* 45, no. 1 (2010): 144-63.

just one incarnation of the Christ.[10] This brought him into line with the high regard for the person of Jesus Christ, and indeed, strong devotion to him, which has characterized much Hindu religious thinking since the late nineteenth century. Jesus' social teaching in the sermon on the mount was widely admired, most famously by Mahatma Gandhi. What is most challenging to Christology in India was that many gave Christ a status comparable to the *avatars*, the incarnations of gods such as Krishna or Vishnu.

Two questions must be asked. What kind of 'divinity' is incarnated in an *avatar*? And what understanding of humanity is implied? We have to say that an understanding of the divine very different from that found in the ancient traditions of India emerged from Christian Theology. In contrast to those traditions, the Triune God of Christian faith is not only 'personal' but Tri-personal in such a way that God is inherently and eternally a relational community of persons. Personhood can therefore only be understood relationally. But as a reflection of that, there has developed in Christian Theology (and in cultures shaped by it) a concept of personhood that profoundly affects our understanding of what it means to be *human*. A greater emphasis on the true and full *humanity* of Christ therefore is vitally important in the development of Asian Christology.

Timoteo Gener notes that there has been a neglect of Jesus' humanity and his servanthood to the poor and marginalized, including women.[11] *Dalit* theology agrees. Reacting against the dominance of dialogue with Brahmin thought in Indian Christian Theology, Arvind P. Nirmal (1936-95) pioneered a school of Christian Theology arising from the Dalits, the so-called untouchables of the caste system. He took a lead from the Liberation Theology of South America and argued that Jesus himself was a Dalit. The humility of the hu-

---

10. Raimundo Panikkar, *The Unknown Christ of Hinduism: Towards an Ecumenical Christophany*, 2nd ed. (Maryknoll, NY: Orbis, 1981), 27.

11. Timoteo D. Gener, 'Christologies in Asia: Trends and Reflections', in *Jesus without Borders: Christology in the Majority World*, ed. G. Green, S. Pardue, and K.K. Yeo (Grand Rapids: Eerdmans, 2015), 59-79.

man Jesus, preaching good news to the poor, mixing with the outcastes, undertaking servile tasks, and broken on the cross, speaks to us today.

Classical Buddhism is particularly concerned with suffering: all life is suffering, according to the first of the four noble truths. Against that cultural background, the focus of Kazoh Kitamori on the 'pain-love' of God resonates in Japan. He begins with the suffering of the human Jesus.

The articulation of the doctrine of Christ in China presents different problems, but here again, thinking about the *humanity* of Christ is vital for the mission of the Church. The Western philosophy of Marxism shaped Chinese thinking and culture in the twentieth century, but the deeper, underlying influence of Confucianism has not been eliminated. Both of these focus on the social and political aspect of humanity rather than the transcendent or the internal spirituality of the individual. K.K. Yeo argues that in this context the Church 'can offer a Christian Chinese Christology (and soteriology) that explains Jesus as the fulfilment of the Confucian ideal of "being human" (*ren*).'[12]

This brief survey of Christology suggests that across the global Christian Church in Asia, Africa, and Latin America, the doctrine of the full *humanity* of Christ is vital in the proclamation and contextualization of the Gospel. This can also be seen as we turn to the contextual theologies of the West.

Contextual Christologies: The West

Feminist Christology is primarily concerned with a *human* issue. Feminism has arisen from the egalitarian and libertarian principles of modernity. It is a reaction against the restrictions and limitations on women and, indeed, the oppression of women in traditional patriarchal societies. Feminist theologians have targeted the masculine language used for God in the Christian tradition. Classical Christian Theology insists that, despite the use of the masculine gender

---

12. K.K. Yeo, 'Biblical Christologies of the Global Church: Beyond Chalcedon?' in *Jesus without Borders: Christology in the Majority World*, ed. G. Green, S. Pardue, and K.K. Yeo (Grand Rapids: Eerdmans, 2015), 174.

to refer to God, God is beyond the division of the sexes and is therefore neither male nor female. But Feminists have argued that the use of the masculine gender for God has shaped our culture and therefore lies behind the oppression of women. Their argument is strengthened by those Christian traditions that try to defend an exclusively male priesthood or ordained ministry by reference to the maleness of Christ.

When it comes to Christology, the more radical Feminism runs up against the stubborn fact that Jesus of Nazareth was male. Since that is the given, it is not surprising in the light of Feminist concerns that the question has been posed how this male can represent the female half of the human race. The underlying issue here for both Black and Feminist Theology is once again what it means to be *human*, and how this relates to 'the scandal of particularity'. One cannot be a human being without being a particular human being, and so clearly, that is also true in the case of the Incarnation. God became incarnate not as a white European, nor as African American, nor as Chinese, nor as Indian, African, or Arab. The offence of the scandal of particularity is that he became incarnate as a Jew. But to say that because he is a Jew, he cannot represent Africans or Europeans or Hispanics or Chinese is quite simply racism. It is the fact that the human race is *one* race, which means that a particular person, Jesus of Nazareth, who was born into the Jewish nation, is able to represent all humanity. And that also has a bearing on the division of the 'sexes' (the word coming from the Latin verb *seco*, I divide). These are not two different races but a division *within* the one human race.

Biblically, the marriage of a man and a woman results in their being irreversibly 'one flesh', thus symbolizing and particularizing the truth that the whole human race is 'one flesh'. 'He made from one [*ex henos*] every nation [*pan ethnos*] . . . on all the face of the earth' (Acts 17:26). Perhaps it is those who have never experienced a labour ward who fail to grasp that! It follows then that while the Son of God did not live on earth as a black woman, a Chinese mandarin, a European nun, or an African slave, that does not mean that he did not enter into the outward circumstances and the inner thought life common to all humanity. He shared our lot, including our temptations 'in all points' (Heb. 4:15, KJV), and he knew not only human life in a family and in the workshop but the common human experience of suffering and dying. In the light of the radical Feminism of Jesus himself in giving women an unprecedented role among his followers, Feminists are right to insist that in Christ 'there is neither male nor female' (Gal. 3:28). But that is an implication of the full and true *humanity* of Christ, including the particularity which that necessarily involves.

Implications of Christology

At the conclusion of this all too brief review of contextual Christologies, therefore, the question has to be raised whether they really contribute anything *to Christology* at all. They are concerned with the *implications* of Christology—and indeed of the Gospel—to particular contemporary human contexts, and that is clearly highly valuable to the ministry of the Church. But to draw out the implications of Christology for mission and ministry is not quite the same as contributing to our understanding of Christology itself. One should expect some feedback from context to doctrine. Each new cultural development should throw a new light on doctrine, but exactly what difference do these contextual theologies make to the Chalcedonian confession, the first authoritative contextualization of the Christology of the New Testament, that the Lord Jesus Christ is fully human, fully God, but one Person? It is not at all evident that they require that basic shape of Christology be changed.

What they may do perhaps is to encourage fuller concentration on the true and full humanity of Christ and the implications of that for the mission and ministry of the Church today. That will have particular implications for the Church's stand on ethical and social issues. But their subtle danger is that they focus our attention on ourselves instead of Christ! The focus of thought becomes *human* need, *human* injustice, *human* sin, the *human* condition, rather than the Saviour who became human in order to save us. The focus becomes our contemporary ideologies rather than the Gospel, and the Gospel is reshaped to *correlate* with the fashionable ideologies.

True, it was in order to save us that he came! But in order to see that, the focus of our attention must not be on ourselves and our own human need, but on him. Of course we must be aware of human need and sensitive to human questions as Jesus was. Our salvation was the purpose of his coming! But our plight needs to be seen in the light of the One who is the solution—the Saviour of the world, our Wisdom, Justice, Sanctification, and Redemption. He *is* our peace. In his Incarnation, he comes right into our human context: but Christ, and not our human context, must be at the centre of our Theology *and our mission*. Christology, understood as the proclamation and worship of Christ, must be central.

Christ Our Sanctification

One other debate about the humanity of Christ deserves our attention. In the last century, attention was drawn to the doctrine of the Christian Fathers that Christ *sanctified* our human nature in his birth, life, and death. This aspect of the doctrine of Christ is often summed up in the saying of Gregory Nazianzen that 'the unassumed is the unhealed.' Nazianzen was responding to the Apollinarian doctrine that the Son of God could not have assumed a human mind, since that was sinful. He made the point, common to all the Fathers, that that was precisely why he *did* assume a human mind as well as a human body!

In recent decades, a debate has become formulated in the question whether Christ assumed 'fallen' or 'unfallen' human nature. That may be an unfortunate way of posing the question, since 'fallen' is equated with 'sinful' and therefore to say that Christ assumed 'fallen' humanity seems to deny his sinlessness. Such an idea is abhorrent to the Christian conscience! The confusion is made worse because one of the first scholars to draw attention to this doctrine in the Fathers, Edward Irving, actually *did* appear to compromise the sinlessness of Christ. The understandable reaction is to say that Christ must have had 'an unfallen human nature'. But clearly, Irenaeus, Athanasius, Gregory of Nazianzus, and the rest of the Christian Fathers were not compromising the sinlessness of Christ. God forbid!

Three points may clarify the matter. First, in using the Chalcedonian language and concept here of human 'nature', we must understand that there is no such thing as 'a' human nature. There is only 'human nature', common to all humankind. Here the Hellenistic concept faithfully conveys the Old Testament understanding of the corporate unity, the solidarity of human 'flesh'. It was that one common human nature which the Son of God assumed in the Incarnation. His humanity was not created afresh from the ground or from anything else! It was *our* humanity he took.

Secondly, that corporate humanity was 'fallen' human nature, meaning that it was subject to both *sin* and consequently *death*. Rejecting the doctrine of the immaculate conception of Mary that developed late in Roman Catholic tradition, we must say that it was the common human nature which the Son of God assumed in his Incarnation from his mother. He was not born with a resurrection body! He was born with a body subject to death so that it could be offered in consecration to the Father. In that sense therefore it was, as mortal, a fallen body, and it was in that body that he was subject to temptation in every way, as we are.

Thirdly, we come to the main point. It was our human nature that the Son *sanctified* by the Holy Spirit, even in conception and birth, so that he was the *sinless* one. His body was mortal but sinless. This sanctification was further pursued through his perfect life. He not only sanctified our common human *flesh* in his birth, but he sanctified our human *life* dynamically in his perfect life in which his *mind* was fully consecrated to the will of the Father. And finally, this sanctification of our humanity was brought to perfection in his sacrificial *death*, burying the old Adamic humanity in his tomb and raising in his resurrection as the first fruits of the new humanity.

What all this means is that the sinlessness of Jesus is not a merely negative thing, a sinless sacrifice offered for us. It was that. But it was more than that! This was not only a legal perfection to satisfy God's holy law. It was a dynamic perfection, a sanctifying of *our corporate humanity* in his mind and heart and soul and body, so that we may be sanctified *in Christ*, as members of his corporate Body by his Spirit. Even though we remain in the fallen, mortal body, falling short of that absolute perfection which is his alone, yet, as we abide in him, we may know in this life victory over sin and a heart fully committed to the will of the Father in the fullness of his Spirit. We are sanctified *in* Christ.

TEN

One Person: Our Lord Jesus Christ

Who is Jesus Christ? In this book, we have traced the development of our Christian understanding of Jesus Christ as Lord. That Christian understanding begins, not with the research of modern historians (though we took note of them in the Prelude), but with the apostles.

In their Gospel, the apostles proclaimed that Jesus is the one who was crucified for our sins and was raised from the dead, appearing to witnesses. The narrative has a 'one-in-two' shape. It is the same One who is *(a)* crucified and *(b)* raised from the dead. Already within the New Testament, this narrative is extended at both ends. It begins with the One who was in the 'form' or 'image' of God, who was the Word of God from before creation, and who became human in what John calls 'becoming flesh' or 'incarnation'. It ends with this same One, exalted and given the divine name, confessed to be 'the Lord' to the Father's glory.

The early Church thus confessed this God as Father, Son, and Holy Spirit. New converts made this confession at their baptism in what developed into the 'creed'. The three articles of belief are in the Father, the Son, and the Holy Spirit, and at its heart is the second article on the Son, including the narrative of the Gospel. This creed was formed in the living worship of the Church in the sacrament of baptism and was eventually given definitive form by the Church councils of Nicaea (AD 325) and Constantinople (AD 381).

Later, to end any continuing confusion or distortion, the Council of Chalcedon (AD 451) added what we might think of as a further footnote, the Chalcedonian Symbol or Definition. It is not another creed: it is a further explication of the second article of the creed. It rules out some misunderstandings, and to do so, it uses the Greek terminology of the day to say that our Lord Jesus Christ is 'One *Person* in two *natures*'. We have to admit that this terminology has always been controversial. What is meant by 'nature' and 'Person'? Where did this language come from? Is it necessary? Is it not misleading?

In the last chapter, we considered the two 'natures'. So finally in this chapter we come to consider what we mean when we confess our Lord Jesus Christ to be 'One Person', and why it is vitally important to say this. Here the emphasis is on the 'One'. But where does the term 'person' come from and what does it mean? And is there not something inherently contradictory about this? How can one Person possibly have two 'natures'? Is this not simply a hopeless contradiction, an illogical nonsense? And how does the term 'person' emphasize the *unity* of the movement.

Beginning with the One-in-Two

The very structure of the doctrine of Christ as 'One-in-two' has given rise in the modern era to talk of 'high' and 'low' Christology and also to talk of Christology 'from above' and Christology 'from below'. Clearly the language of height and depth is being used here as a visual model to help us think about the relationship of deity and humanity within the unity. A 'high' Christology is one that emphasizes the deity of Christ but may or may not be clear on his humanity. A 'low' Christology is one that emphasizes his humanity and will tend to compromise his true and full deity, while perhaps trying to give some explanation of some lesser meaning for 'divinity'.

The terminology of '*from* above' and '*from* below' means something different. These terms refer more to the method we employ, how we come to think of this. They were coined by the German theologian Wolfhart Pannenberg. He claimed that the whole Christian tradition from the Fathers onward began Christology 'from above', adopting a God's-eye view and so beginning with the pre-incarnate Logos who then became flesh. This meant that it failed to do justice to the true humanity of Jesus. Instead, Pannenberg argued that, in view of the Enlightenment, we must begin 'from below'. The historical-critical method could establish Jesus' true humanity as a figure in human history—and could even establish the historicity of his resurrection. Thus belief in Christ could be rationally established.

It may appear that this is the order that has been followed in this book. We began with the scholars who have tried to establish the truth about the 'historical Jesus' and, through our study of the historical questions about the resurrection, came to the confession of Jesus Christ as Lord. But the two chapters on the search for the 'historical' Jesus were deliberately called a 'Prelude'. Historical research is a purely human endeavour that can lead us to the threshold of faith. But it cannot take us over the threshold! Our own reasoning does not bring us all the way to faith. Faith is the gift of God. Our own insight as historians may help us, but it cannot be the basis of our faith.

Christology does not begin therefore with either of the 'two'—either 'from above', that is, with the deity, or 'from below', that is, with the historical humanity. Our faith only begins at that moment when we kneel before Christ and confess, 'My Lord and my God!' Faith begins with the recognition of the One-in-two. The 'given' is not the humanity alone or the deity alone. What we are given is the proclamation in the Gospel that in Jesus Christ, these 'two' are 'one'. To recognize and know Jesus Christ as Lord is therefore not our own achievement or insight. It is only when the Spirit gives us the ability to recognize him as Lord that we know who Jesus is. It is only by grace. In other words, theology is not intellectually proving the Christian faith to be true. It is rather 'faith seeking understanding'.

We must also add this. To respond in faith to the Gospel narrative of Christ's death and resurrection is already to listen to the witnesses, that generation, centred in the Twelve, who were witnesses to his life, death, and resurrection and who proclaimed him to be 'Christ the Lord'. There is no way to faith in Christ except through the Gospel, the apostolic witness of the New Testament.

That leads us then to this question. If the one-in-two Saviour is given to us in the one-in-two Gospel, the narrative of his descent all the way to the cross and grave and of his exaltation to glory, what then is the role of the Church's Chalcedonian Symbol or Definition? How far is it necessary today to confess the faith in the language and concepts used at Chalcedon?

Chalcedon as a Model

It has been helpfully suggested that we should look on the Chalcedonian Symbol as a 'model'. All our language is in fact sign language, unavoidably shot through with metaphors and other figures of speech. A 'model' is *a key metaphor*, and the use of 'models' is common to all academic disciplines, including the natural sciences. In the era of classic Newtonian physics and cosmology, the universe was widely thought of as a vast mechanism, rather like a clock. That was a 'model', a definitive metaphor. Later, when James Clerk Maxwell was struggling to understand electro-magnetism in the mid-nineteenth century, he suggested the model of the magnetic 'field'. It was not a matter of each distinct part acting causally on another distinct part, as in Newton's physics. It was rather that the 'field' as a whole was a reality that makes the parts (such as iron filings round a magnet) move in the way they do.

But both of these are *models*: the universe is not literally a machine or a field! Such models are essential to scientific thinking and method because they are the ways in which we apprehend reality and express our thinking. Like all metaphors, models are partly alike and partly different from the realities to which they refer. A metaphor is the comparison of two *different* things with respect to some way in which they are *similar* so that one always has to take account of the *dissimilarities* as well as the *similarities*. But metaphors do enable us to say what we otherwise could not say.

Theology, and indeed the language of Scripture, is highly metaphorical. Jesus was not literally a shepherd or a door or bread or a gate or indeed a lamb. This metaphorical language is not just incidental but provides us with definitive *models*. A key one is the model given to us by Jesus himself when he spoke to and about God as 'Abba, Father'. At this point, we must be careful to insist, however, that *metaphors are not fictions*. Metaphors are ways of referring to what is true in reality. God is not literally our male parent, but he is, in a true and real sense, 'Our Father'.

It is important to see then that the Chalcedonian Symbol presents us with an elaborate *model* for the doctrine of Christ. As a model, it is a set of metaphors drawn from late Hellenistic culture, dominated as it was by the traditions of Platonism and the categories and logic of Aristotle. It is not itself the Word of God in Holy Scripture. Rather, it was an attempt by a major council of the Church to give some definition to the Church's doctrine of Christ, contextualizing it in the culture of the day. It did not claim to define Christ, but to define what must *not* be said about him, ruling out the distortions that had sprung up in the course of contextualizing the Gospel, in order that the truth of the Mystery of Christ might be confessed and adored.

As a model, the Chalcedonian Symbol has what we may call an 'internal logic', but to understand this we have to examine the Greek words it uses. If we do not take that trouble, we simply will not understand it. These key Greek words had already been used in debates about the doctrine of the Trinity.

The Word 'Person'

First, there is the word 'person'. In fact, the Chalcedonian Symbol uses two Greek words, *prosōpon* and *hypostasis.* The literal root meaning of *prosōpon* is 'face', what we present to others in relationships 'face-to-face'. The Latin Fathers used the equivalent Latin word, *persona,* often referring to the face or mask that actors wore in classical drama. It was through (*per*) the mask that they sounded (*sonare*) their words, and the word came to refer to a 'role' in a drama. But the Greeks were afraid that this word on its own left the implication that Father, Son, and Holy Spirit only assumed different roles temporarily. So they added the word *hypostasis,* meaning 'underlying reality'. God did not just temporarily appear to be Father, Son, and Spirit. He really was so from all eternity.

These two words, *prosōpon* and *hypostasis*, were now applied to the Son for the first time officially in the Chalcedonian Symbol. Our Lord Jesus Christ truly was a distinct 'Person', God the Son, from all eternity. But note that the word *prosōpon* did not mean 'person' in the way we use it today, meaning a separate individual with his or her own inner psychology. God is not three individuals! God is indivisible—one Individual. Rather, the word 'person' was being used to mean One who has his being in relationship, face-to-face with the Father in the Spirit. The word *hypostasis* emphasized that this was not merely temporary appearance, but that this is who he was from all eternity. From all eternity, the one indivisible God has his being in three face-to-face 'Persons' in personal communion with each other. Our Lord Jesus Christ is one of these three divine 'Persons'.

The Word 'Nature'

Secondly, there is the word 'nature'. As the Latin word *natura* comes from the word 'born' or 'come into being' (*natus*), so the equivalent Greek word, *physis*, was a noun coming from the verb 'to be born' or 'to come into being' (*phyomai*). A word with a slightly different meaning sometimes used as a synonym was *ousia*, 'being', coming from the present participle of the verb 'to be'. Our human 'nature' is thus the consequence of our *birth* from human parents. All humankind shares in the same common human 'nature' or 'being'. So the word is also used by analogy for God (even though God never came into existence!) to say that Father, Son, and Holy Spirit share the same 'nature' (*physis*) or 'being' (*ousia*).

What was now said at Chalcedon, using the terminology already worked out for the Trinity, is that our Lord Jesus Christ is one divine 'Person', eternally God in 'nature' and 'being', who has now assumed a second 'nature', human 'nature', by being *born* (*natus*) of Mary. He did not unite another 'person' to himself: that would mean that there were two persons in the God-man. That is to say, there was not a babe already in the womb before being assumed into union. Rather, the babe only came to be conceived because this one divine Person assumed common human 'nature' into union with himself. He did this in such a way that our common human nature now had a new personal centre 'in' the Person of the eternal Son of God. The consequence is the birth of that human being, Jesus, who was already God while still in the womb of Mary. At this point we pause for a few moments in awe and wonder to worship!

A Paradoxical Model

It is important to see that the Chalcedonian Symbol is not trying to explain this. Rather, it is trying to rule out misunderstandings. It gives us a paradoxical model and not a logical explanation. To do so, its language is drawn from the Aristotelian scheme differentiating between the 'being' or 'substance' (*ousia*) of something and its accidental properties. One problem for us is that this Aristotelian way of thinking was rejected as meaningless by the empiricist philosophers of the Enlightenment. 'Substance' referred, said John Locke, to 'a something I know not what'. This makes it important to see that the Chalcedonian Symbol does not give us a 'picture model' which fits in every respect, but a 'disclosure' or 'analogue' model that 'fits' to some degree but is inappropriate in others. The model is not the reality itself, and there are points where it does not 'fit' the reality.

These are sometimes presented as logical objections. One example is the objection that Chalcedon gives us a kind of Apollinarianism. So, where Apollinarius denied that Christ had a human mind, so the Chalcedonian model, following Cyril of Alexandria, denies that he had a human *hypostasis* or person. But the error there is to think that we can divide the human being in a Platonist way into parts. Rather, following the Old Testament understanding, the human being is a psychosomatic unity. The 'person' or *hypostasis* is not a part of a human being, but who that human being is.

Another example is the objection that to speak of two natures in one person is a 'category confusion' and self-contradictory. The very word 'category' reveals that the objection comes from someone thinking within the Aristotelian system. But the more substantial reply is that in order to find the union of deity and humanity 'contradictory' we have to be able to define both terms. It is doubtful, however, whether we can give a full definition of what 'humanity' is, and it is even clearer that we cannot provide a 'definition' for divine nature. To define is to set limits (*fines*), and it is therefore inherently contradictory to think that we can define the *infinite* God.

Repeatedly, the Fathers had to rebuke heretics who thought that they could apply human logic to God. Gregory Nazianzen denounced the extreme Arians as 'talkative dialecticians' who thought that they could use Aristotelian logic to prove that, since God was by definition the 'Unbegotten' or 'Unoriginate', the Son could not be God, since he was the 'Begotten'. Cyril of Alexandria denounced the Nestorians because they insisted on following Aristotelian logic. They argued that human 'nature' could only appear in specific instances (*hypostaseis*) so that we must speak of two 'persons' (*hypostaseis*) in Jesus Christ. Cyril insisted that the terminology must not dictate to the reality or 'truth' of Christ which was beyond our logic. There is a point therefore at which our 'kataphatic' theology (*kata phasin*, according to speech) must give way to 'apophatic' theology (*apo phasin*, beyond speech).

That implies that, although we must not use paradox as an excuse for lazy thinking, in the end of the day, once we have explored the capabilities of our models, we have to admit that no linguistic or logical scheme can capture the reality of the God-man. The paradox of the Incarnation is not an actual or real contradiction. We are incapable of defining 'deity' and 'humanity' sufficiently to be able to say that. To speak of paradox is rather to say that it may *appear* to be a contradiction, but that actually it is the best we can do to express the inexpressible and to articulate the Mystery.

Conundrums

The paradoxical nature of the doctrine of the Incarnation is also to be seen in specific conundrums that are sometimes raised. Was it possible for Christ to sin? Some, starting from his deity, have said that since God cannot sin, Christ could not have sinned. He was 'impeccable'. Others have said with the Antiochenes that if it was impossible for him to sin, he did not face genuine temptation, therefore he was not genuinely obedient, and so he could not have achieved our salvation. That implies the staggering thought that God loved us so much that he even risked his own integrity and deity in order to save us. Actually, this is an unavoidable part of the paradox. Insofar as Christ was true God, it would seem that he could not sin: insofar as he was truly human, it would seem that he could sin. There we have to leave it. This is beyond our understanding, and we cannot push this any further.

Similarly, this applies to the three standard attributes of God developed in the classical theism of Aquinas—omniscience, omnipotence, and omnipresence. Was Jesus omniscient, omnipotent, and omnipresent during his years on earth? Different viewpoints have been presented, including, as we noted, views of the kenoticists such as P.T. Forsyth. But once again, it is better to regard this conundrum as part of the paradox. We really do not know how the mind of Christ worked, whether at two levels—divine and human—or one: and we really do not know whether he temporarily laid aside his omnipotence or whether he was in full possession of this attribute while among us but voluntarily limited its use in day-by-day obedience to the Father.

Once again, while we are to push as far as we can in understanding the doctrine, in the end Christian doctrine cannot contain God or the God-man. We can only confess with the apostle: 'Great is the Mystery of godliness: Who was manifested in flesh, vindicated in Spirit, seen by angels, proclaimed among the nations, believed on in the world, taken up in glory' (1 Tim. 3:16, author's translation). Appealing to mystery is not avoiding the issue, as a proud rationalist might think: it is the very point from which we have to begin if we really want to pursue genuine Theology concerned with the true and living God. We begin, that is, from our ignorance and our total dependence on God's revealing just as much about himself as he will.

'Person', Not 'Individual'

Having examined the logic of the unity of the Person of Christ, uniting true deity and true humanity in himself, we must now examine more fully the key word that was adopted at Chalcedon from the Church's Trinitarian vocabulary to express that unity, the word 'person'. Given that God has revealed himself in the *Person* of his Son, and given that we can only understand this as we are enlightened by the Holy Spirit, how does this word 'person' help us to express this? What is the significance of speaking of the one 'Person' of Christ? How does this help us with the 'who?' question with which we have been wrestling, 'Who is Jesus Christ?' Can this word, 'person', made official Church language by the Council of Chalcedon, help us to articulate our confession of who he is? What is this non-biblical concept of 'person' that we are employing, and how should we understand it in a way that draws out the implications of Holy Scripture?

We have acknowledged that the word 'person' is not used in Scripture in this way, but we can trace the modern concept to Christian roots. Most people will come to the discussion with the common assumption that a 'person' is by definition 'a human being'. That is indeed what the word has commonly come to mean. And we think that we know what a human being is. In fact, the humanities and human sciences are centred on the human being. We are fascinated by ourselves! Characteristically, in the modern era we have equated a human 'person' with an 'individual'. And the modern concept of the individual has developed from the ancient Hellenistic concept of 'the soul'.

Some contemporary philosophers still defend the classical notion of the soul, derived from Greek thought and traditionally read into Scripture. By contrast, the Hebrew word for 'soul', *nephesh*, refers to the 'life' of the body rather than to a distinct substantive entity. But while most modern thought has ceased to think in terms of the Greek concept of soul, what has survived from that is the notion of the *individual*. The root of modern individualism can be seen to lie in the ancient Greek notion that souls have existed and will exist eternally as separate monads who only temporarily inhabit a body.

While the Hellenistic concept of the soul has largely disappeared from modern secular thought, its legacy is still with us—*individualism*. Persons are defined as individuals who have intelligence, consciousness, and will. They are thought to be independent agents who must be free to think and believe and, most importantly, to choose. But that is not what the word 'person' means in Christian Theology. There are some points of similarity of course, but to understand what is meant by the 'Person' of Christ, we must begin with the fact that the word 'person' was not used in the ancient world of Greece and Rome, nor indeed in Israel, to refer to individual human beings. The word simply does not appear in the Bible or in ancient philosophy with that modern meaning.

But the concept of 'person' that developed first in Christian Trinitarian Theology does not mean a stand-alone individual, one whose being is that of an isolated, self-sufficient monad whose relationships are purely optional and voluntary. On the contrary, the Father, the Son, and the Holy Spirit are three 'Persons' *whose very being is constituted by their relationships.* The Christian God is not three individuals, but three 'Persons' who together constitute one *indivisible* God—one 'Individual'! The concept of 'person', in contrast to the concept of the 'individual', is an inherently *relational* concept. It was only at Chalcedon in AD 451, however, that the words *hypostasis* and *prosōpon* became the official language of the Church by being included in the Chalcedonian Definition.

Modern Usage

What does it mean then to say that the Lord Jesus Christ is one 'Person'? We must avoid reading into this word all the modern developments that make 'person' the equivalent of 'individual'. Nor must we confuse 'person' with 'personality', a psychological construct used to classify and categorize. Further, the modern concept of consciousness or self-consciousness was not part of the original theological meaning of the word. But one of the clear implications of the early history of the word within Christian Theology is that when we say that Christ is a 'Person', we mean that we can only understand *who* he is when see him within a context of *relationships.* And we see these relationships acted out within the drama, the narrative of the Gospel and the fuller narrative of Scripture.

Before we pursue that thought, it will be instructive to sketch the development of a philosophical and theological movement known as 'Personalism' in the nineteenth and twentieth centuries. It has deep roots. Two influential thinkers at the end of the patristic period can be seen to have shaped later developments. One was Augustine, who introduced a focus, notably in his *Confessions*, upon the interior life. That was to have a long-term influence on the concept of the 'person'. The other thinker was Boethius (c. 480–524), who gave this definition: 'a person is an individual substance of rational nature.' This definition of the human 'person' essentially as an 'individual' strongly promoted that tendency to equate 'person' with 'individual'. The original theological understanding of the 'person' as constituted by relationships was absent. Boethius defined the 'person' as an 'individual' in a most *impersonal* way!

The modern movement of Personalism can be seen as embracing Augustine's development of the concept of the person as involving the interior life of consciousness and self-consciousness, but rejecting the individualism of Boethius for a more relational understanding of personhood. It appeared in two forms: more strictly as a metaphysical system and more widely in several schools of thought that overlap and combine with other philosophical developments.

In the strict sense, Personalism as a metaphysic was developed from the thought of the German thinker Rudolph Hermann Lotze (1817-81) by the American Borden Parker Bowne (1847–1910), Methodist minister and professor of Philosophy at Boston University. But more widely, a variety of schools of thought may be regarded as 'Personalist' because they rejected impersonal systems. While not developing a whole metaphysic like Bowne, they wanted to accord persons a significant place in their ethics and general outlook. The influence of Personalism in this wider sense can also be seen in the thinking of (among others) such different thinkers as Martin Buber (1878–1965) and Michael Polanyi (1891–1976).

Buber is noted for his 1923 work *Ich und Du*, in which he differentiated between the personal reciprocal relationship a subject has in *encounter* with another subject ('I and Thou') and the way in which a subject acts upon an impersonal object ('I and It'). For Buber as a Jewish thinker, the former, 'I and Thou', characterized one's relationship with God. Michael Polanyi, the Hungarian scientist who developed a whole epistemology as a philosopher of science, demolished the notion of high, modernistic rationalism that science was a totally objective pursuit. In his Gifford Lectures, published as *Personal Knowledge* (1958), he developed the view that all knowledge required a personal subject to do the knowing as well as an object to be known.

This wider Personalism is rooted in the Judaeo-Christian tradition, but shared by many who are not orthodox Christian believers. While a Jewish thinker such as Martin Buber saw personal interaction between human beings and God in the narratives of the Old Testament, the full development of the concept of the person has arisen from Christian Trinitarian Theology. With that brief characterization of this modern fruit of Christian Theology more generally in the European philosophical tradition, we can more readily appreciate the new, modern and postmodern significance of understanding our Lord Jesus Christ as a 'Person'.

Persons in Relation

The theologian T.F. Torrance has drawn on the insights of this thinking about 'persons' to elucidate what we mean when we speak of the 'Person' of Jesus Christ. In his Didsbury Lectures,[1] Torrance notes a significant comparison between Christian Theology and the development of modern science. Since James Clerk Maxwell and Albert Einstein, modern physics has developed a relational way of thinking. Whereas the old classical physics of Newton thought *analytically*, dividing physical reality into discrete entities that then interacted, since Clerk Maxwell and Einstein, scientists have thought more *holistically*. Thinking begins not with discrete separate entities that are then thought to interact, but with the 'field' in which they are found already related to each other.

---

1. These significant lectures were given at Nazarene Theological College, Manchester, in 1982 and published as *The Mediation of Christ* (Exeter: Paternoster, 1983). Citations are from the expanded 2nd edition (Edinburgh: T&T Clark, 1992).

Torrance draws a comparison with the way theologians and biblical scholars have treated Jesus. They have *analyzed* the biblical narratives into smaller units (*pericopae*) and then have tried to join them together artificially. They have tried to see Jesus as a mere man and then to explain how he was accorded the status of God. Instead we need to think more holistically. We must understand Jesus in the context of his given *relationships*, first, his relationship to Israel, and secondly, his relationship to God.

The One True Israelite

Thinking of Jesus in relation to Israel, we see that before we could understand what God was doing in the life, death, and resurrection of Jesus, we needed 'conceptual tools', adequate modes of thought and speech. Those 'tools' were forged by God in advance of his coming through the history and institutions of Israel. Like Jeremiah's potter throwing the lump of clay on the wheel, or like a father shaping his children, God imprinted himself on Israel through the centuries, shaping a whole set of spiritual tools. This was a harrowing experience, bringing intense suffering to Israel.

Torrance illuminates the way in which Israel was thus elected by God to form a 'community of reciprocity' within the covenant. God's revelation of himself through Israel has thus provided 'permanent structures of thought and speech about him.' Torrance lists these, referring to 'the Word and Name of God, to revelation, mercy, truth, holiness, to messiah, saviour, to prophet, priest and king, father, son, servant, to covenant, sacrifice, forgiveness, reconciliation, redemption, atonement, and those basic patterns of worship which we find set out in the ancient liturgy or in the Psalms.'[2] Without these 'conceptual tools', we could not express our Christian faith.

But Torrance emphasizes that the covenant relationship which God established with Israel was more than a means of abstract conceptual revelation, for revelation is inseparable from *reconciliation*. We cannot know God without being reconciled to him. 'Knowing God requires cognitive union with

---

2. Torrance (1992), 18.

him in which our whole being is affected by his love and holiness. It is the pure in heart who see God.'[3] The foundations of the covenant partnership were clear: 'You shall be holy, for I am holy' (see Lev. 19:2; 20:7, 26).

But Israel, like all peoples, was a sinful people. The covenant was established in pure grace, not with a people who were already holy, but 'between God and Israel in its sinful, rebellious and estranged existence.'[4] But, as the book of Hosea insisted, God would not divorce Israel. The validity of the covenant did not depend on Israel's fulfilment of contractual conditions, but on the unconditional grace of God. The love of God provided a vicarious way of response in the liturgy of atoning sacrifice. But 'the closer God drew near, the more the human self-will of Israel asserted itself' so that the closer God came, the more Israel's sin was intensified.[5] This was not accidental, but God's intention, for only in this way could God effect reconciliation with humanity *at its worst*.

That is the context for the Incarnation in which God drew so near that God and humanity are one in Jesus, *Emmanuel*, 'God with us'. What Torrance wants us to see is that the 'deep-seated human estrangement from God became the very means used by God in actualising his purpose of love to reconcile the whole world to himself.'[6] Without Israel's great sin in rejecting the Messiah, there would have been no crucifixion, and therefore no Atonement, no forgiveness, no sanctification, no resurrection, and no hope of eternal life. The point is *that God used our very sin, focused in Israel's rejection of her Messiah, as the means of our redemption*. That means that the relationship between Jesus and Israel, representing us in committing the greatest sin of all, has been irreversibly established once and for all. We are each free to deny that and be eternally lost, but we cannot change the fact that, in the Mediator, God united himself irreversibly to the human race, providing salvation for us all.

---

3. Torrance (1992), 26.
4. Torrance (1992), 27.
5. Torrance (1992), 28.
6. Torrance (1992), 32-33.

One with God

Having explored Jesus' oneness with Israel, Torrance turns again to the other aspect of his twofold strategy, to explore Jesus' oneness with God. The 'Person' of Christ—*who he is*—cannot be understood only by examining his relationship with Israel. Even more basic is his relationship with the God of Israel, the One he uniquely called 'Abba, Father'.

The 'basic clue' with which the early Church theologians worked, therefore, was the Father-Son relationship. Matthew 11:27 (paralleled in Luke 10:22) was particularly important, that 'no one knows the Son but the Father and no one knows the Father but the Son.'[7] This mutual and exclusive relationship in the Holy Spirit (Luke 10:21) falls, Torrance emphasizes, *within the very being of God.* The implication is that this Person, constituted by his relationship with the Father in the Holy Spirit, who through his Incarnation has now entered into onto-relations with us, is uniquely qualified not only by what he does *but by who he now is* to be the Mediator between God and humanity.[8]

He is not merely 'God in man' but 'God as a man.' He is not merely the agent or instrument of the mediation: he *is* the mediation. He *is* the Word: he *is* the Truth: he *is* our Peace. It is not just what he *does* for us in dying for our sins: it is *who he is for us* which gives what he does for us its basis and foundation. This is absolutely vital for the coherence of the Gospel. Only if this is so, Torrance points out, is Jesus' forgiveness of sins not merely the word of a fellow creature but the forgiveness of God himself. 'But cut the bond of being between Jesus Christ and God, and the bottom falls out of the Gospel of forgiveness.'[9] If there is no oneness of being between Jesus and God, then we no longer have a secure ground for claiming that God is love. If there is a gap between Jesus and God, then we have

---

7. Torrance (1992), 53.

8. 'Onto' comes from the Greek word 'to be', and 'onto-relations' is Torrance's word for relations which constitute our being—that is, 'being-constituting relations' (Torrance [1992], 47).

9. Torrance (1992), 58.

no assurance that the love Jesus shows throughout his earthly life is the true revelation of a loving God.

Personal Relationship with Jesus Christ

Torrance therefore wrote of our Lord Jesus Christ as 'the personalizing Person'. It is through *relationship* with him that damaged humanity can be transformed into truly *personal Persons*. Building upon Torrance's work here, we may finally explore the way in which Jesus' *personal relationships* during his life on earth are integral to his work as Mediator. We are not neutral philosophers examining some theories from a detached, disinterested, and neutral stance. To qualify as theologians at all, we have to be Christian believers, committed to this Person, the Lord Jesus Christ. Only those who know God in Christ are qualified to speak of him, for no science can be based on ignorance and lack of experiential contact. We are therefore not merely recycling second-hand academic knowledge about Christ. We begin with our first-hand encounter with him, *Person to person*.

That is why the reading and exposition of the stories of the four Gospels is so central to Christian worship and the Christian life. The risen exalted Christ, alive today in the presence of the Father, comes and encounters us by the Spirit in the reading and exposition of Scripture. It is here in Holy Scripture, where we read the accounts of the witnesses who recalled their stories of Jesus under the inspiration and guidance of the Holy Spirit that we are brought face-to-face with Jesus. After his baptism and temptation in the wilderness, Luke tells us, he came 'in the power of the Spirit into Galilee' (Luke 4:14) and proclaimed his mission in the synagogue in the words of Isaiah, 'The Spirit of the Lord is upon me' (Luke 4:18). He encounters the sick and heals them, he liberates those bound by demonic possession, he heals the lepers, and he even raises the dead. All of these are personal encounters in his teaching, preaching, healing ministry (Matt. 4:23; 9:35) where his astounding compassion moves us.

He calls his disciples—James and John, Andrew and Peter, and Levi, challenging them to follow *him*, to commit themselves to the journey without knowing where it may lead in sheer personal commitment to *him*. He tells his masterly stories—the Prodigal Son, the Lost Sheep, the Workers in the Vineyard, the Good Samaritan—puzzling and provoking us to thought, questioning our assumptions about God and about life. He challenges us to turn the other cheek and go the second mile, to build our house on the rock and not the sand. He challenges Zacchaeus and the rich young ruler to give up their riches and commit themselves to *him*. He flares up in indignation at the proud and hypocritical, denouncing the 'whited sepulchres'. He affirms the law of God but rescues the adulterous woman from stoning. He speaks kind but straight words to the woman at the Samaritan well. He speaks of justice and righteousness and peace and the coming of the kingdom. He champions the poor, the outcasts, and the lepers. He throws parties for sinners.

We follow him on the way of the cross as he sets his face as a flint toward Jerusalem. We shout 'Hosanna' with the crowds. We see him furiously expelling the money changers from the temple. We hear those last public teachings, the six royal riddles, the prophecy of the fall of Jerusalem, the barbed parable about the death of the son of the owner of the vineyard. We hear him say that he came to serve and 'give his life as a ransom for many' (Mark 10:45). We are admitted to the upper room where through the eyes of John we see him washing the apostles' feet and speaking of his Father and the Spirit. Through the ears of Peter and his account given to Mark, we hear him speak of the blood of the covenant and see him transform the Passover meal into the Communion in his body and blood. We are awestruck as he stands before Caiaphas and Pilate, distraught as we see him mocked and flogged, alarmed as he stumbles on the way to Golgotha, dumbfounded as he is nailed to the cross, moved as he forgives his torturers, and confused and despairing as we hear him crying out, asking why God has abandoned him. With the disciples, hope is dead within us.

But that is not the last encounter. With Mary we are mystified at the empty tomb, but with the apostles we encounter the risen Lord in the locked room. With Cleopas and his companion we listen on the road to his exposition of the Hebrew

Scriptures, and with speechless awe, we bow with Thomas back in the upper room and hail him as the Resurrection and the Life, 'My Lord and my God!' (John 20:28). So, through the accounts of his earthly life and ministry, the present exalted Christ speaks to us again, and in the personal encounter we are called to confess him as Lord, to acknowledge our sins before him, to receive the forgiveness won through his cross. We listen to his voice of guidance for our lives today, transmitted through his own teaching while here among us in the flesh and through the writings of the prophets and his appointed and commissioned apostles.

So for us, it is not a matter of 'religion' or 'religious practices' that express our own piety. It is not a matter of a set of doctrines or theories, or a philosophy of life. It is not at its heart a matter of joining an institution or following a tradition or campaigning for a cause, although it may involve all of those. It is not even just a matter of seeking salvation and security in the afterlife. At its heart, it is a matter of personal commitment to *a Person*. It is personal faith and trust in him, issuing in glad obedience. Christianity is Christ. Everything else follows from this relationship of personal commitment to this Person in life and death.

Who is Jesus Christ? He is Lord. He is *the* Lord, God the Son, who took human flesh, died for our sins, and rose again. He rules from the Father's throne, and he will come again to establish his kingdom in glory. This is our confession and proclamation. This is the One we have come to know in the fellowship of his Church. He is our hope in life and in death.

Bibliography

Athanasius. *On the Incarnation of the Word*. Pages 36-67 in vol. 4 of *Nicene and Post-Nicene Fathers*. Second Series, edited by Philip Schaff and Henry Wace. 1892. Reprinted, Peabody, MA: Hendrickson, 1994.

Barrett, Lee C., III. *Kierkegaard*. Nashville: Abingdon, 2010.

Barth, Karl. *Church Dogmatics*. Vol. 1, *The Doctrine of the Word of God*, pt. 2. Translated by G.T. Thomson and Harold Knight. Edited by G.W. Bromiley and T.F. Torrance. London: T&T Clark, 1956.

Bauckham, Richard. *God Crucified: Monotheism and Christology in the New Testament*. Carlisle, UK: Paternoster, 1998.

———. *Jesus and the Eyewitnesses: The Gospels as Eyewitness Testimony*. Grand Rapids: Eerdmans, 2006.

———. *The Testimony of the Beloved Disciple*. Grand Rapids: Baker, 2007.

Bebbington, David. *Evangelicalism in Modern Britain: A History from the 1730s to the 1980s*. London: Routledge, 1989.

Behr, John. *Irenaeus of Lyons: Identifying Christianity*. Oxford: Oxford University Press, 2013.

Bindley, T. Herbert. *The Oecumenical Documents of the Faith* (1899). 4th ed. London: Methuen, 1950.

Bockmuehl, Markus. 'God's Life as a Jew: Remembering the Son of God as Son of David'. Pages 60-78 in *Seeking the Identity of Jesus: A Pilgrimage*, edited by B. Gaventa and R. Hays. Grand Rapids: Eerdmans, 2008.

Bonhoeffer, Dietrich. *Christology*. London: Collins, 1966.

Brunner, Emil. *The Mediator: A Study of the Central Doctrine of the Christian Faith*. Translated by Olive Wyon. London: Lutterworth, 1934.

Calvin, John. *Institutes of the Christian Religion* (1559). Translated by Henry Beveridge. 1845. Reprinted, Grand Rapids: Eerdmans, 1989.

Cone, James. *A Black Theology of Liberation.* Maryknoll, NY: Orbis, 1986.

Crosby, Fanny J. 'To God Be the Glory'. No. 36 in *Sing to the Lord.* Kansas City: Lillenas, 1993.

Cullmann, Oscar. *The Christology of the New Testament.* London: SCM, 1959.

Donaldson, Terence L. 'The Vindicated Son: A Narrative Approach to Matthean Christology'. Pages 100-121 in *Contours of Christology in the New Testament,* edited by Richard N. Longenecker. Grand Rapids: Eerdmans, 2005.

Dunn, James D.G. *Christology in the Making: An Inquiry into the Origins of the Doctrine of the Incarnation.* London: SCM, 1980.

———. *Unity and Diversity in the New Testament: An Inquiry into the Character of Earliest Christianity.* London: SCM, 1977.

Evans, C. Stephen. *Passionate Reason: Making Sense of Kierkegaard's Philosophical Fragments.* Bloomington, IN: Indiana University Press, 1992.

Fee, Gordon D. *Pauline Christology.* Peabody, MA: Hendrickson, 2007.

Flemming, Dean. *Contextualization in the New Testament: Patterns for Theology and Mission.* Downers Grove, IL: IVP, 2005.

Forsyth, Peter T. *The Person and Place of Jesus Christ.* London: Hodder and Stoughton, 1909.

Gener, Timoteo D. 'Christologies in Asia: Trends and Reflections'. Pages 59-79 in *Jesus without Borders: Christology in the Majority World,* edited by G. Green, S. Pardue, and K.K. Yeo. Grand Rapids: Eerdmans, 2015.

Gregory Nazianzen. Epistle 101. Pages 439-43 in vol. 7 of *Nicene and Post-Nicene Fathers.* Second Series, edited by Philip Schaff and Henry Wace. 1894. Reprinted, Peabody, MA: Hendrickson, 1994.

Gwatkin, Henry M. *Studies of Arianism.* 2nd ed. Cambridge: Deighton, Bell, 1900.

Hall, Stuart G., ed. *Melito of Sardis: Pascha and Fragments.* Oxford: Clarendon, 1979.

Hardy, Edward R., ed. *Christology of the Later Fathers.* The Library of Christian Classics. Philadelphia: Westminster, 1954.

Harnack, Adolf von. *What Is Christianity?* London: Williams and Norgate, 1904.

Heaney, Sharon E. *Contextual Theology for Latin America: Liberation Themes in Evangelical Perspective.* Carlisle, UK: Paternoster, 2008.

Hick, John. *God and the Universe of Faiths.* London: Macmillan, 1973.

———. *God Has Many Names.* Philadelphia: Westminster, 1980.

———. *An Interpretation of Religion: Human Responses to the Transcendent.* New Haven, CT: Yale University Press, 1990.

———, ed. *The Myth of God Incarnate.* London: SCM, 1977.

Holmes, Stephen. *God of Grace and God of Glory: An Account of the Theology of Jonathan Edwards.* Edinburgh: T&T Clark, 2000.

Hurtado, Larry. *Lord Jesus Christ: Devotion to Jesus in Earliest Christianity.* Grand Rapids: Eerdmans, 2003.

———. *One God, One Lord: Early Christian Devotion and Ancient Christian Monotheism.* Minneapolis: Augsburg Fortress, 1988.

Ignatius. *The Epistle to the Ephesians.* In *The Epistles of St. Ignatius, Bishop of Antioch,* translated by J.H. Srawley. London: SPCK, 1919. https://www.google.com/books/edition/The_Epistles_of_St_Ignatius_Bishop_of_An/H0j5ENyBdNkC?hl=en&gbpv=1.

Irenaeus. *Against Heresies.* Pages 315-567 in vol. 1 of *Ante-Nicene Fathers,* edited by Alexander Roberts and James Donaldson. 1885. Reprinted, Peabody, MA: Hendrickson, 1994.

———. *Proof of the Apostolic Preaching.* In *St. Irenaeus: Proof of the Apostolic Preaching,* translated by Joseph P. Smith. Ancient Christian Writers 16. Westminster, MD: Newman Press, 1952.

Kärkkäinen, Veli-Matti. *Christ and Reconciliation.* Vol. 1 of *A Constructive Christian Theology for the Pluralistic World.* Grand Rapids: Eerdmans, 2013.

Lull, Timothy, ed. *Martin Luther's Basic Theological Writings.* Minneapolis: Fortress, 1989.

McIntyre, John. *The Shape of Christology: Studies in the Doctrine of the Person of Christ.* 2nd ed. Edinburgh: T&T Clark, 1998.

Melito of Sardis. *Peri Pascha.* In *Melito of Sardis: Pascha and Fragments,* edited by Stuart G. Hall. Oxford: Clarendon, 1979.

Panikkar, Raimundo. *The Unknown Christ of Hinduism: Towards an Ecumenical Christophany.* 2nd ed. Maryknoll, NY: Orbis, 1981.

Pannenberg, Wolfhart. *Basic Questions in Theology.* Vol. 1. London: SCM, 1970.

Plantinga, Alvin, and Nicholas Wolterstorff, eds. *Faith and Rationality: Reason and Belief in God.* Notre Dame, IN: University of Notre Dame Press, 1983.

Pope, William Burt. *A Compendium of Christian Theology*. 3 vols. 2nd ed. London: Wesleyan Conference Office, 1879-80.

———. *A Higher Catechism of Theology*. London: Woolmer, 1883.

———. *The Person of Christ: Dogmatic, Scriptural, Historical*. London: Wesleyan Methodist Book Room, 1874.

Reed, Rodney, and Gift Mtukwa. 'Christ Our Ancestor: African Christology and the Danger of Contextualization'. *Wesleyan Theological Journal* 45, no. 1 (2010): 144-63.

Rose, Tim. *Kierkegaard's Christocentric Theology*. Aldershot: Ashgate, 2001.

Schleiermacher, F.D.E. *The Christian Faith*. Translated by H.R. Mackintosh and J.S. Stewart. Edinburgh: T&T Clark, 1928.

Tertullian. 'To Scapula'. Pages 105-8 in vol. 3 of *Ante-Nicene Fathers*, edited by Alexander Roberts and James Donaldson. 1885. Reprinted, Peabody, MA: Hendrickson, 1994.

Thomson, Robert W., ed. and trans. *Athanasius:* Contra Gentes *and* De Incarnatione. Oxford: Clarendon, 1971.

Torrance, T.F. *The Mediation of Christ*. 2nd ed. Edinburgh: T&T Clark, 1992.

———. *Space, Time and Resurrection*. Edinburgh: Handsel Press, 1976.

Tyrrell, George. *Christianity at the Crossroads*. London: Longmans, Green, 1913.

Wesley, John. *The Works of John Wesley*. Vol. 18, *Journals and Diaries I (1735-1738)*, edited by William R. Ward and Richard P. Heitzenrater. Nashville: Abingdon, 1988.

Wiley, H. Orton. *Christian Theology*. 3 vols. Kansas City: Beacon Hill Press, 1940-43.

Wright, N.T. *Jesus and the Victory of God*. Vol. 2 of *Christian Origins and the Question of God*. London: SPCK, 1996.

———. *The New Testament and the People of God*. Vol. 1 of *Christian Origins and the Question of God*. London: SPCK, 1992.

———. *The Resurrection of the Son of God*. Vol. 3 of *Christian Origins and the Question of God*. London: SPCK, 2003.

Yeo, K.K. 'Biblical Christologies of the Global Church: Beyond Chalcedon?' Pages 162-79 in *Jesus without Borders: Christology in the Majority World*, edited by G. Green, S. Pardue, and K.K. Yeo. Grand Rapids: Eerdmans, 2015.